academic writing is...

A GUIDE TO WRITING IN A UNIVERSITY CONTEXT

TERRI MORLEY-WARNER

Copyright © Terri Morley-Warner 2009
Reprinted with corrections 2010
Reprinted 2016

First published in three editions by CREA Publications
This edition published by the Association for Academic
Language and Learning

This work is copyright. Apart from any fair dealing for the
purposes of private study, research, criticism or review as
permitted under the Copyright Act 1968 and subsequent
amendments, no part may be reproduced, stored in a retrieval
system or transmitted by any means or process whatsoever
without the prior written permission of the publishers.

Copying for educational purposes
Copying for educational purposes is permitted by law under
Part VB of the Copyright Act, subject to adherence to prescribed
procedures. Further information is available from the Copyright
Agency Limited.

National Library of Australia Cataloguing-in-Publication entry:
   Morley-Warner, Terri, 1947-
   Academic writing is : a guide to writing in a
   university context / Terri Morley-Warner.
   ISBN 978-0-9804297-2-5 (pbk.)
   Includes index.
   Bibliography.
   1. Academic writing – Handbooks, manuals, etc.
   2. Dissertations, Academic – Handbooks, manuals, etc.
   3. Report writing – Handbooks, manuals, etc.
   Association for Academic Language Learning.
   808.066

Cover and book design by Jo Morley,
Humming Studio, *www.hummingstudio.com*

Set in ITC New Baskerville Std
Printed in Australia

contents

preface	6
introduction	7

1. academic writing is ... understanding what is expected — 9

what makes writing academic?	10
being clear about your purpose	13
being clear about your audience	13
getting the 'right' tone	14
being critical	15

2. academic writing is ... understanding your writing process — 17

managing time and place	18
recognising stages in the writing process	20
stage 1. interpreting the task: what & how?	
stage 2. researching & reading	
stage 3. thinking & sorting to get to a plan	
stage 4. drafting & editing	
stage 5. polishing & proofreading	
paragraphing	26
topic sentences and signal words	27
cohesion	28
exam essays	29
choosing the text-type – essay or report?	30
last draft checklist	32

3. academic writing is ... writing the essay — 33

establishing a clear structure:	34
the introduction	
the body	
the conclusion	
writing the body of the essay by recognising purpose	37
the expository essay: the essay that informs	
» description	
» explanation	
» comparison-contrast	
the discussion essay: the essay that argues & evaluates	
» argument, analysis & critical analysis, critical evaluation	
model discussion essay	45
checklist	48

4.
academic writing is ...
writing the report
49

purpose and audience	50

recognising types of reports:
    experiential
    information
    research
	51

strategies for starting a report	53

sections of the report
    introduction
    body
    » method / methodology
    » findings / results / data
    » discussion / analysis
    conclusion
    » recommendations / implications
	53

using graphical material: figures and tables	58
reference list and bibliography	59

supplementary parts / endmatter
    glossary & list of acronyms
    adding an appendix
	59

checklist	60

5.
academic writing is ...
making it 'sound' academic: tone and style
61

levels of academic writing	62
writing from a personal perspective	64

writing from an academic distance
    what comes first in a sentence
    verb choice
    pronoun choice
    active or passive construction
    abstract nouns
    technical terms
    nominalisation
    tentative tone
	65

getting the balance	70
combining personal and distanced writing	70
objectivity?	71

6. academic writing is … text types — 73

the abstract and the executive summary	74
the annotated bibliography	75
the case study	76
the critique (critical evaluation, critical analysis)	78
the literature review	79
the reflective journal	81
the research review	82

7. academic writing is … referencing — 83

why reference?	85
what to reference	85
how to reference	86
in-text citations	
footnote or endnote citations	
primary & secondary sources	
online sources	
paraphrasing	89
giving direct quotes	90
integrating evidence	91
avoiding plagiarism	92
compiling a reference list and bibliography	93

8. academic writing is … proofreading — 97

common sentence level problems	98
incomplete sentences	
agreement of subject & verb	
consistency in use of pronouns	
pronouns & sexist language	
verb tense	
apostrophes	
common misspellings and spelling strategies	103

a final word	105
bibliography	111
appendix	116
index	117

preface

This new edition of ***academic writing is ... a guide to writing in a university context*** has been made possible by the Association for Academic Language and Learning, and has been prompted by considerable encouragement from students and lecturers about its usefulness, both on Australian campuses and overseas. It is gratifying to learn that it has found a place in some academic language and literacy classrooms, and in fact, some readers have passed it to their children in senior high school or TAFE, a wider audience than I first envisaged.

The book retains the principal themes of previous editions and the many reprints that ensued since it was first published by the Centre for Research and Education in the Arts, University of Technology, Sydney in 2000. This edition now includes revised examples and greater reference to the influence of electronic communication, an indication of the times in which we live.

If asked to define academic writing in a word, I would choose clarity: so why then an entire book dedicated to explaining what academic writing is? The answer would have to be that achieving clarity is a complex matter in an academic context because it involves demonstrating knowledge and understanding, structuring material logically, making appropriate language choices for a specialist reader and authenticating claims with reference to research and theory. All of this is overlaid with an expectation for critical analysis and reflection. No wonder that some students have defined academic writing as frustrating, even as 'a nightmare' and that some of their teachers have admitted to despair!

But it can be done, and this book attempts to explain how. Assertions about the writing process, genres and strategies are well supported by research which can be found in the bibliography, and my own position in the debates about academic literacy is outlined in an essay at the conclusion of the book. Claims are also supported by my own experience as a writer - as a student, a researcher, a teacher and finally as a senior lecturer at UTS. Listening to and talking with students in many stages of their academic writing careers – from undergraduate to doctoral level, training to be teachers, nurses, engineers and business people – I have appreciated their frankness in sharing their frustrations and successes as they learned to 'do' academic writing. This has been an invaluable resource for this book, and hopefully their questions are answered in these pages.

My thanks also to the staff from diverse faculties at UTS who have shared their beliefs and concerns about their students' writing, on which I draw here, and especially to my colleagues in the ELSSA Centre, UTS, for all those conversations about writing. In particular, I wish to thank Alex Barthel, Director of the ELSSA Centre and President of AALL for his efforts in bringing this new edition to a new audience of students Australia-wide.

Thanks, Sue, for your hard work; Jo, for making this edition look so special, and as always, thank you Neville for your endless patience and support.

Terri Morley-Warner, August 2009

introduction

reading this book

This book attempts to demystify the practices of academic writing for students in an Australian university at the present time. How to write academically and meet the expectations of the lecturers who are assessing you through your writing is a major concern for many students. In particular, those who are returning to study after some time away are often concerned about 'getting it right'. Students with English as a second (or third or fourth language) often are concerned about their grammar, and about finding out how it is 'done' in an Australian university context. Students coming to university straight from school may have had recent practice in essay writing, particularly for exams, but may not have experienced some of the different types of assignments required in the university, and may find significant differences between the expectations of high school writing and writing at the tertiary level.

An important definition: Throughout the explanations, the term **text** is used to refer to any meaningful piece of writing, print or electronic. For example, this book is a long and systematically arranged text, while any notes you take about writing (on paper or computer) are likely to be short and abbreviated texts. A quick email, blog or SMS to another student about an assignment would also be called a text, even though it may be very colloquial and unconventionally spelled. (The term is generally used for any spoken message as well: a lecture may be a formal and structured text while a phone conversation is often a more spontaneous and fragmented text.)

This book is organised to answer questions that students frequently ask. You can use the Contents page or the Index to select particular sections that you may need for particular assignments. Explanations and examples are generic rather than discipline-specific, in order to draw attention to the **how** of the writing rather than the content. Cross-references have been provided throughout the text to guide you to related sections, as of course many aspects of writing overlap (for example, proofreading is needed at many stages). Margin notes provide extra information or a quick summary, and you may also find the margins useful for your own notes.

→ *How do I know what is expected?*
    Part 1 examines expectations and assumptions about academic writing that may be current in the university. This includes being clear about your purpose and audience for a particular assignment, and understanding issues of style and tone to meet those expectations.

→ *What can I learn about academic writing?*
    Part 2 explores the writing process for assignments and exams, providing useful strategies for each stage: from managing your time and study place, interpreting the task, researching and reading, thinking it through, sorting and planning your material with suggestions about brainstorming and mind-mapping, to drafting, editing and proofreading. It examines paragraphing

as the key to planning and the usefulness of the topic sentence and signal words in writing cohesively. This section also answers general questions if you have to choose a text type for a learning contract or major study.

→ *What is an essay?*
Part 3 focuses on the usual structure of the essay. Essay writing for different purposes is explained with specific strategies for planning the logical development of your material and making it flow. Detailed strategies are suggested for writing a description, an explanation, a comparison or a discussion. A model discussion essay is outlined.

→ *What is a report?*
Part 4 examines the basic structure of a report, explaining the purpose of each section and its language conventions, whether writing about an experience or from research. How to include graphics and an appendix is also covered.

→ *What does academic writing 'sound' like?*
Part 5 explains when it is acceptable to write in a personal manner, and when you need to be aware of writing in a more distant and formal tone. This section provides examples and explanations of how to change the wording of a sentence to make it more abstract and 'objective'.

→ *What is expected from particular types of assignments?*
Part 6 summarises the purpose, structure and language expected in a variety of texts: the abstract (and executive summary), the annotated bibliography, the case-study, the critique (and critical evaluation), the literature review, the reflective journal and the research review.

→ *What is referencing and how do I do it?*
Part 7 addresses common questions and misunderstandings about referencing procedures and compiling a reference list or bibliography. It also explains plagiarism and how to avoid it. It focuses generally on explaining conventions with detailed examples, and is not intended to replace careful reading of specific faculty or university guidelines.

→ *What should I proofread?*
Part 8 outlines proofreading strategies to enable you to recognise common sentence-level errors, the 'always-with-us' problem of the apostrophe and some typical spelling demons.

→ *A Final Word*
The author explains her position regarding advising students about academic writing in a short essay, demonstrating how the above parts come together.

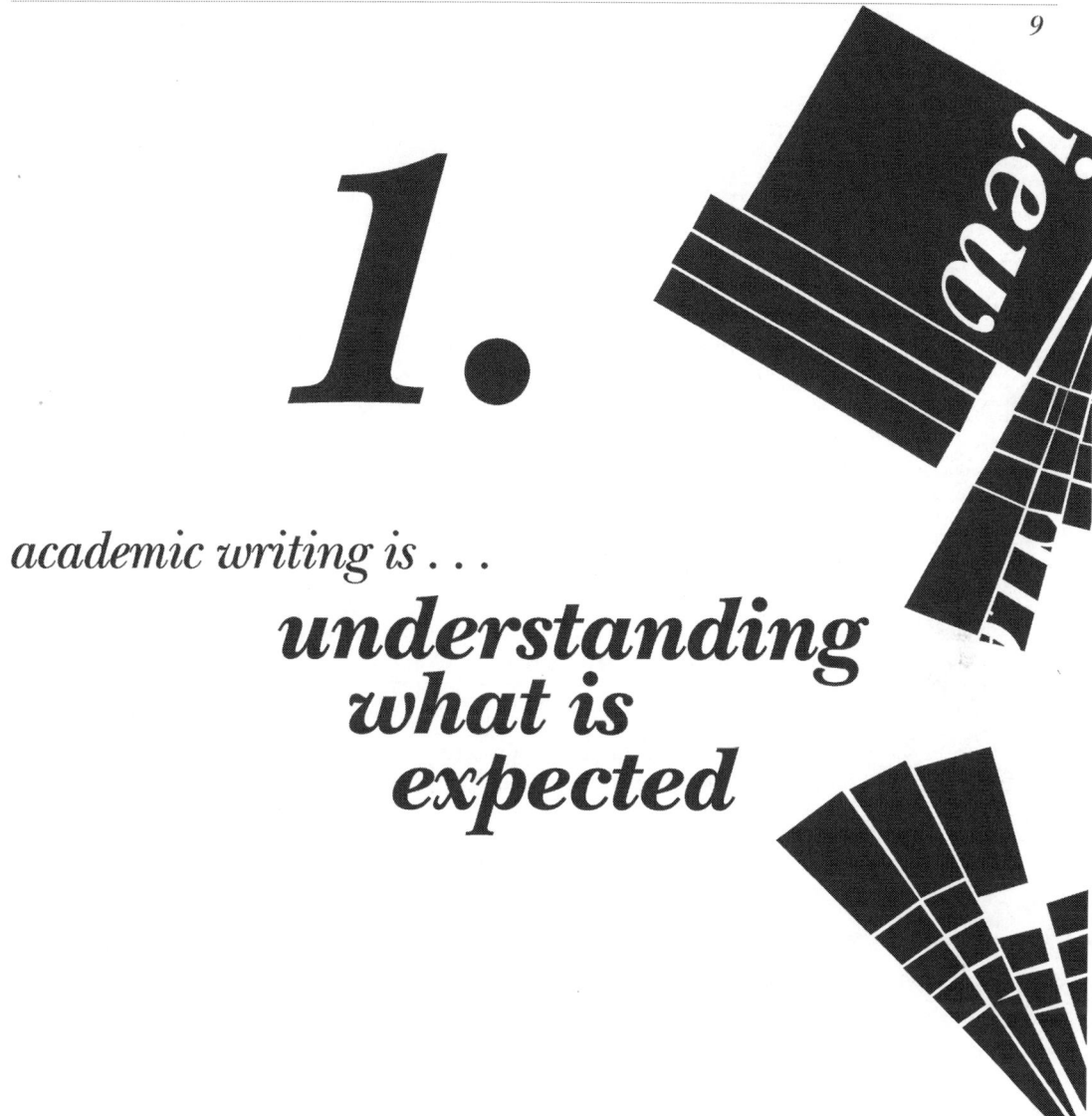

academic writing is . . .
understanding what is expected

what makes writing academic?

being clear about your purpose

being clear about your audience

getting the 'right' tone

being critical

what makes writing academic?

understanding the university culture

The university is a culture in itself; a particular place where particular customs are followed, where 'rules' can be invisible and how things are done is often taken for granted. In fact, it may be more accurate to describe the university as a collection of cultures, with variations across faculties, courses and subjects, and it is not uncommon to find significant differences in the expectations of lecturers within the same academic grouping. It is realistic to be aware of variations in expectations as you move from faculty to faculty, course to course, and even from lecturer to lecturer. This is particularly important where you may be studying a subject that crosses several disciplines. An engineering subject focussed on issues of the environment, for example, crosses into sociological, environmental and historical areas where traditions of writing are quite different to science and applied subjects.

repertoire: all the different ways that you can write

You may need a repertoire of writing practices as you move from one subject to another where different expectations operate. These variations are inevitable when there may be different reasons for setting a particular assignment and where different fields of study are embedded in different traditions of writing: one task may be intended to test students' ability to argue from evidence, for example, and another to ensure in-depth reading for comparisons of ideas. The emphasis of a particular assignment thus depends on the intentions of the person setting it, so that you need to learn to 'read' these expectations by listening carefully to any additional comments that may be made about the assignment by the lecturer or tutor in class. Ask questions!

In particular, read closely the assignment's instructions and any additional explanatory notes which may accompany it. Read the objectives set out for the subject to see if you can relate the assignment to its overall goals: for example, is this assignment pitched at developing your critical skills, or is its purpose to get you to understand how a particular theory offers an explanation for what occurs in the workplace? Again, if you are not clear about what an assignment wants you to do, ask!

Some students have few problems adapting and learning to meet expectations, especially if university work resembles other learning experiences. However, for many it may mean a collision of different writing practices, perhaps requiring them to un-learn previous ways of writing to accommodate the assumptions of what makes 'good' writing in a particular academic context. Frequently students who write as part of their job in the workplace feel confused when they are expected to write more at university, not less; to expand points with explanations and argument when what may be valued in the workplace is a concise listing of points in phrases or single words, and where elaboration is not desirable. Students whose first language is not English may also find difficulty understanding the expectations of writing in a different culture while at the same time coping with the eccentricities of English grammar and idiom.

Some students may have become competent in short-answer responses to questions, or in writing examination essays which are inevitably first drafts written under the pressure of time. In contrast, when assignments are set throughout a semester as a form of on-going assessment, it is expected that time will have been spent researching and re-writing a number of drafts, and that evidence of that research will be given to substantiate an argument. It is also expected that the assignment will have been carefully proofread, eliminating spelling, typing and grammatical errors and ensuring that referencing conventions are consistently applied. The 'one-off' text written right on a deadline can rarely manage all these requirements. Strategies for overcoming many of these difficulties can be found throughout this book.

In general, if a sweeping statement can be made about academic writing in all its range of text-types, it is that academic writing at this time and place is expected to be:

predictable:

your thesis is your point of view

The writer's purpose for the task and his/her point of view (or thesis) are clear from the start and the assignment proceeds to provide information, argument and evidence to support that thesis. The introduction to an essay or report makes the text that follows predictable. Similarly, the abstract or executive summary of a report ensures predictability. It also operates through the structure of the assignment by the use of topic sentences and signal words in paragraphs.

see Part 2, 3, 4 and 6

connected and cohesive:

There is a 'flow' of information and ideas that makes sense to the reader in a logical sequence. Again, the text structure becomes explicit with the use of topic sentences and signal words in paragraphs.

substantiated:

expository texts are texts that explain and inform

Evidence, examples and explanations for the writer's critical analysis and claims are provided.

Some expository tasks require you to research and explain a process or an event. Some assignments ask for and value your own experiences, requiring you to analyse your personal experience in the light of your reading so that you show how a particular theory might explain an experience. Many tasks want you to demonstrate wide reading on a topic or issue, and then to critically evaluate what you have read, by comparing and contrasting the various ideas or findings from your reading. In all these cases, you are expected to support your assertions and strengthen any argument by reference to the research or theories of others in your field.

You can see that these factors make academic writing unlike other types of written text: a novel for example, where events may unfold unexpectedly, or a letter to a friend where irony may be used for humour. The factors which tend to identify academic writing in a university at this time are derived from the history of western tertiary education that we have inherited, which includes rhetorical or stylistic devices such as 'pretending' that the reader/tutor does not already know the information; where it is considered essential to provide an overview at the beginning of the writing and a summing-up at the end; and where the body of the writing is expected to provide the reader with connected and logical information, well-substantiated by research. How to do this is explained in detail with examples in Parts 2 to 8.

This does not mean that there are not other ways to write academically.

Other cultures set up different expectations and train their students to write differently. For example, some may require lengthy introductions to establish an appropriate writer-reader relationship; others expect a solid reliance on quoting from experts and some do not permit the use of the personal 'I' or 'we' in any academic writing. However events change conventions and students have to learn new ways of writing in preparation for their careers.

changing conventions }

The most significant 'event', and hence, challenge to traditional conventions of academic writing, is the rapid development of the electronic 'information' age. Its impacts are considerable: there is an abundance of Internet material that requires critical reading and skill in editing, with increased possibilities of plagiarism. The globalisation of economies requires common understandings of texts across cultures and languages. The growth of off-campus courses, for example, may challenge the traditional essay as the most useful form of assessment, requiring interactive modes of writing and new means of communicating. Some researchers suggest that digital technologies such as e-mail, blogging and sophisticated tools for media production set up different conventions for writing that have a place in the academy. Meanwhile, even at the mechanical level of writing, the computer is changing some traditional punctuation conventions (e.g. not indenting for a new paragraph, removing full-stops between a writer's initials and the apostrophe in a company's name) and increasingly Americanising spelling. Frequently such changes are resisted and debated in the *Letters to the Editor* section of newspapers or by radio commentators. However it is clear that students in this electronic context need to learn a repertoire of skills in order to switch from one type of text or mode to another, and to be flexible and adaptive.

Further, some tasks may be set that require you to write for a virtual audience other than the actual reader (your lecturer or tutor) much like in a role-play scenario, such as a submission to a government department; clinical notes for a nursing manager; a lesson plan for an adult migrant English class; Web pages for a client and so on. Such tasks may require specific models other than the academic conventions explained in this book, so you should follow faculty or school guidelines; as a writer you need to recognise the appropriate language to use for disparate tasks.

ask questions

To sum up, it is important to understand **what** is expected of you as a student, in this context. If you try to understand the new culture/s in which you find yourself, you may find it easier to meet these expectations. Realising that within the university culture there may be different, even conflicting, expectations of your writing may help you to feel encouraged to ask questions that clarify just what is wanted in a writing task. Therefore, you need to be conscious of **why** you are writing a particular assignment, and **who** you are writing it for. This may sound commonsense but an unclear idea of the purpose and audience for the writing often causes problems. Critically analysing the who, what and why of academic writing makes the **how** of it a skill that can be learnt.

see: being critical }

text construction

It also helps to understand that writing assignments for university is about constructing texts, that is, building up a text from raw materials (the research and reading) in response to the requirements of someone else (the lecturer), unlike many other writing practices where you write for your own purposes (such as a personal or business letter or email), or creative writing where your imagination may flow freely. See Part 2.

To write successfully at university you need a sense of what the final product should look and 'sound' like, so if possible, read model assignments or if these are not available, study the way in which journal articles have been written in your specific area. These articles may be lengthy and some may be based on research rather than a discussion of issues, but from them you will get a sense of how academic writing 'sounds', that is, its tone, and also how respected writers in your field assemble information. You will gain a sense of the complexity of being an apprentice writer in an academic culture, or rather cultures, where expectations may vary from discipline to discipline, even subject to subject and where you can build a repertoire of critical thinking and writing skills that enable you to enter the academic debates, even to challenge. See Part 5.

being clear about your purpose

Obviously you are writing the assignment to get marks so that you pass the course and if possible, to get credits, distinctions, even high distinctions in the subjects. You may have plans to move on to a higher degree. It is essential to be very clear about the specific purpose of each writing task: what is it you have been asked to do? Once you have researched the subject, are you clear what it is that you are expected to do with the material? It is not enough to merely present it on the page as evidence of your hard work. You need to ensure that you are following the instructions of the task carefully. For example, if you are asked to *compare*, or *explain*, or *justify*, you need to organise the information that you have researched accordingly. Further, it is important to analyse the task so that you use the evidence you have gathered from your research and reading to make a point, to argue for a point of view or for a particular explanation. See Part 2.

being clear about your audience

the intelligent stranger }

*explicit:
being clear and
leaving nothing
implied*

Clearly the audience for your assignment is the person marking it, who obviously knows a lot about the subject. This sometimes leads to confusion as student writers may feel that they do not need to tell **everything** to someone who already knows it! However the assessor expects to be shown that **you** know the material, and that you are able to perform the particular task (an explanation or discussion of it, for example). It may help to think of your writing as **teaching** the reader about the topic, so that by the end of your assignment they will have a clear understanding of it. Do not assume that the reader already knows. Instead, view the reader as an intelligent stranger to the subject. Therefore you are explaining your thinking on the subject and you are demonstrating how ideas are connected or contrasted. Be quite explicit. It is important to define key terms as you use them in an assignment. Even if readers disagree with your definitions, at least they will be clear about your particular frame of reference.

see: word count, Part 7

In this way, your message will be clear and you will avoid the danger of leaving things out because you assume they are too obvious to mention. The word count specified for the task is also an indication of how succinct, or how expansive, the text is expected to be. Writing more than the specification will not usually give you extra marks and may in fact be penalised. Relevance is the key, and careful editing the way to ensure it.

Expect comments on your writing as you may learn through the dialogue that may be set up in the margins of your work. Do not be deflated by critical comments for if you knew everything already you would not need to be here! If no written feedback is provided, it is a useful practice to discuss your assignment with the marker if possible, and ask any questions you may have so that you can improve the next piece of writing. Alternatively, you could take the assignment to an academic writing adviser for comment.

It is essential to proofread assignments carefully, imagining the intended reader (that intelligent stranger) and checking that meaning is clear. Writing is not like a conversation where you are present in person to 'fill in the gaps' should the audience have a question (has the assessor written questions in the margin such as 'what do you mean?'). A written assignment needs to be seen as an independent construction that should make sense without the writer being present to give extra explanations. It should be able to stand alone – which means terms should be clearly defined and the structure should be easy to follow. See Parts 2 and 3.

getting the 'right' tone

Students are frequently concerned to know if they are writing in an 'academic' tone or style, yet it would be impossible to reach a consensus among academic staff about what the 'right' tone is. In fact there is a range of expectations about the tone of assignment writing. It largely depends on the nature and purpose of the task, and the particular lecturer's requirements, usually determined in part by the specific discipline, and by the type of writing found in scholarly journals in that discipline and in professional forums. In other words, it is often said that through assignments, students are learning to write 'like a psychologist' or 'like a historian' and so on (although that suggests there is only one sort of psychologist or historian!). They may also be learning to write for their profession as some students go on to write for scholarly publications and/or for the workplace. Within a discipline there may also be different tasks which require switching to a different tone, structure and vocabulary, such as writing a report for a company, then writing its marketing material. It is essential that you understand the purpose of the text and its expected – even if imagined – audience. See Part 5.

an issue of appropriateness – you and your reader

Within the range of text types (for example, the argumentative essay; the case study; the report) there are different expectations regarding the steps or stages of its structure and the appropriate language and tone; however, you need to be alert to variation between and among disciplines. See Part 6.

The issue of appropriateness relates to the **relationship that you set up as a writer towards your reader**. You may write in a personal tone, which essentially positions you in a familiar style, or in an impersonal tone, which

Plain English — distances you from the reader by more formal writing. Tone also relates to communicating in technical language or in Plain English, depending on the assumptions being made about your audience; however you will always be expected to write clearly.

how will we do this? — Explicit advice on analysing your writing to achieve the desired tone or style and how to make particular choices in wording can be found in Part 5: *making it 'sound' academic*. It is important to have the time to fine tune your drafts so that you achieve the required tone.

suggestions for managing your time follow in the next section — From research it has become clear that for many writers, the act of writing itself helps thinking. That is, as you write, what you think may become clearer **to you**. There is a temptation to try to have it all worked out in your head before starting to write, as if the writing is only for the completed product, as in an exam. In fact, if you view writing as a constructing process, you will see the value of using the drafting process to help you to clarify your ideas. As you draft, keep in mind the purpose and audience for the assignment and try reading your drafts aloud to yourself or others, to become more aware of the tone of the writing and get feedback. See Parts 2 and 5 for suggestions.

being critical

Being critical and writing an argument in an academic sense does not mean being negative, as in an everyday context; for example, *My friend is a critical (fault-finding) person who always argues.* A critical reading may reveal the strengths and possibilities of an interpretation and it is important to balance the positive features with the negative. Writing an academic argument means having a point of view that considers and evaluates other points of view.

Critiquing a novel, a public policy document, a practice in the classroom, an action in the workplace, or someone's theory or explanation will mean evaluating (finding its value); balancing its advantages or positive features with its shortcomings. Check for assumptions, things that may have been taken for granted by the writer. Check for stereotypes and sweeping generalisations and beware of statements starting with *all* and *every*: have these assertions been supported with evidence or reasoning, or are they the product of lazy thinking?

Occasionally students are concerned about how to be 'critical' and it may seem daunting at first to 'criticise' or 'critique' a theory or a practice; however a starting point is to read what others have written about it. You may end up feeling confused – but that is part of the process as you think things through. Evaluate the theory or practice in the light of your own experience as well but do not stop there, as everyone's experience is obviously limited.

Nevertheless your experience **is** a valuable place to start: do you find the idea logical, sensible, reasonable? If you find that you agree without difficulty then you may need to examine why! Perhaps your assumptions coincide with the writer's and so you have no trouble in finding their ideas 'natural' or 'commonsense'. All the more reason then to try to imagine this viewpoint from the perspective of someone who is not the intended reader.

being critical

Examine the following contentions. Do you **immediately** agree or disagree with any of them?

1. *Women's place is in the home.*
2. *Greed is good and competition is natural.*
3. *Engineers have a responsibility to the environment.*
4. *Children need discipline.*
5. *Boys have better technical skills than girls; girls are better at relationships.*

Now question yourself. Where did that immediate reaction come from?

» What do you think may be the origin of your values in regard to this statement – what experiences, whose influences?
» Who would make each claim? Why? How would age or gender, race or culture influence a viewpoint on each statement?
» Who might have a reason to disagree? Why?
» Have people always believed this statement to be true? Can you think of a time or a place where this view would have been held, or would not have been held?

To be a critical thinker means trying to identify your own position and its origins. Consider whether you might change your views in the light of new thinking and reading. For example, how would an 'alternate' reader respond – someone who is older or younger than you? a person from a different cultural background, race or gender? These issues are particularly significant when studying the cultural practices of our society (who or what is 'our'?). Part 3: *planning to write a discussion* gives strategies for preparing this type of text.

2.

academic writing is . . .
understanding your writing process

managing time and place

recognising stages in the writing process
    stage 1. interpreting the task: what & how?
    stage 2. researching & reading
    stage 3. thinking & sorting to get to a plan
    stage 4. drafting & editing
    stage 5. polishing & proofreading

paragraphing

topic sentences and signal words

cohesion

exam essays

choosing the text type – essay or report?

last draft checklist

you as a writer

writing is work!

It is important to analyse yourself as a writer. Is it a task you enjoy or avoid? Something you know you will set about methodically, or leave to the last minute? Attitudes to writing may well stem from earlier experiences, for instance at school, or from current experience in the workplace. It may help to view assignment writing as work; something that has to be planned for in the same way as a task for which you are being paid! To do the work efficiently, you need to know yourself as a writer. What is the best time of day or night for you to work? How do you deal with interruptions and distractions? How do you deal with the pressure of a deadline?

Research comparing the practices of proficient writers with less-proficient writers indicates that the former plan more, and change their plans more readily; that they re-read often during writing and revise more, giving more time to revising content than form. They are said to write reader-based prose, that is, they are more aware of their audience. With this in mind, here are some strategies that may help you to feel more comfortable with the process and put you in control. Each writer has to work out a process that satisfies them, but it is clear that the process takes time, and some time management strategies follow below.

View the process of assignment writing as a series of messy drafts that move closer towards the final product to be submitted. This can also help overcome writer's block, which refers to the experience of finding it difficult, even impossible, to begin writing. Knowing that you are writing a draft which can be changed can relieve the pressure, and serves an important purpose in giving you a text to work on and amend as further ideas develop.

managing time and place

time

timetable each stage of the process

Begin by analysing the demands of each day/evening of the week on a timetable or spreadsheet so that you have a clear view of time available.

The drafting process itself requires timetabling so that there is sufficient time for editing, re-editing and proofreading before submitting the final version. Frequently, students leave little time for this process and even though they may have spent several weeks researching and reading, they do not do credit to this effort because they rush the writing. A conscientious student may also over-extend the research stage because it is interesting and there always seems to be just one more resource to read. Again, this effort is lost if you rush the writing. Use your diary to

diary

note down not only when your assignments are due but when you need to begin drafting, perhaps working out a time to get feedback and booking an appointment with an academic writing adviser, or a meeting with fellow students to discuss progress so far. Setting a deadline for drafting will also help to ensure that you move on to the next stages.

buffer zone

A useful strategy for scheduling your preparation is to build in a 'buffer' zone: that is, make sure that when you have finished the assignment, you still have a day or a weekend left free before you have to hand it in. This time may save you a lot of stress in the event of unexpected dramas, like a computer malfunction!

best time/worst time?

It may be helpful if you can work out your 'best time' for writing each day or week, that is, the time when you feel productive and are not too tired or easily distracted. Use the 'dull' times (if you have them, most of us do!) for library or online searches, for photocopying or sorting and filing notes – don't use your best time for these less demanding tasks. Some students find they are most productive early in the morning, or later at night; you need to work this out for yourself so that when you are analysing or organising your ideas, your brain is at its best. If there are distractions in your study environment, you may need to adjust your week so that you utilise the weekend instead of the weeknights, or vice versa, and work around the distractions.

alternative times?

place

Part of the writing routine should also be that you establish a working space where you can leave your writing in progress, rather than having to pack everything away at the end of a session. Circumstances might make this difficult if you are sharing space, but many students have found inventive alternatives – like a suitcase under the bed that becomes a study centre, or a small folding table in a corner of your room. Many students have found that using the dining room table, where the work must be cleared away, often makes it harder to get started the next time. Writing an assignment from the comfort of an armchair or bed can also be a problem if your body is getting messages to relax and unwind! A desk and office-type chair that make you feel like you are working are probably better alternatives. Some students find that this means that they have to schedule more time at the library where the atmosphere is more conducive to work. Your local municipal library, a TAFE library or another university's library may be closer to home. Also check the campus for dedicated workstations where you can connect your laptop or access a wireless hotspot.

alternative places?

at the ready

If you have your own study space at home and you can leave your work 'at the ready', you may find that when you get an idea it is easy to jot it down, and that even half an hour spent writing may be very valuable. When you are away from your desk, use a notebook (electronic or paper), laptop or mobile phone to record any sudden inspirations you may have. Often a good idea may turn up when least expected as your brain has been mulling things over while you are engaged in a mundane task (see *thinking and sorting* below).

routine

Setting up a routine for writing can make it easier to settle into the task, and also family and friends will come to know that you are working and not to be disturbed. Interruptions and distractions make it very hard to follow a train of thought, and may also make you feel increasingly exasperated or anxious. Stress can certainly block your writing process.

do not disturb!

It has been shown that one of the biggest distracters is television. Clearly, those who inhabit the television set are highly paid to attract your attention. Bright lights and colour, attention-grabbing sound and tantalising action all make it very hard for you to concentrate on writing your assignment! Better to avoid it altogether; if possible, record your program and reward yourself after a period of sustained writing by watching later. In this way you may also find that you can unwind from the taxing business of writing. Any talk on the radio will obviously also compete for your brain's attention.

music?

Many students find that listening to music helps their concentration and this is an individual matter. Often music can drown out other more distracting sounds that may be around, such as the chatter of other students, the neighbours' crying baby or barking dog. If, however, you find that you are paying attention to the music to the extent of listening to the lyrics or thinking about it, then you may have to admit that it is interfering with your concentration. Again, if there are distracting sounds in your study environment, you may need to consider studying elsewhere – at a friend's (as long as he/she is not too distracting!) or at a library.

recognising stages in the writing process

It is not a tidy, linear process – images of the inspired writer from whose talented fingertips the words just flow need to be seen as romantic wishful thinking. For most of us, it is hard work and messy!

1. *interpreting the task: what & how*
2. *researching & reading*
3. *thinking & sorting to get to a plan*
4. *drafting & editing*
5. *polishing & proofreading*

Most writers agree that composing or constructing a text is 'messy' and that they move back and forth between researching, planning, drafting and revising, then going back to an earlier researching stage, then redrafting and revising again.

It is useful, however, for the purposes of this book, to describe the writing process in stages and to think about what you do in each stage, particularly if you have any problems in writing an assignment. Each writer will probably develop an individual approach to writing as more experience is gained. What follows is a way to get started, so that you become aware of useful strategies. Do what works for you!

what works for you?

stage 1: interpreting the task: what & how?

The language of a subject cannot be separated from its content, and learning to communicate confidently in your field requires an understanding of how meaning is made in that field. To help you to interpret the requirements of an assignment, consider that there are two jobs that you have to do: firstly **analyse** what content you need to demonstrate that you understand, and secondly, be sure that you **organise** your writing as required by the task.

what content is required?

What information or data do you need to read about or research? What part of the subject does this task relate to? This will be found by analysing the task for its **key terms**: those words that identify the topic or issue.

metacognition: thinking about thinking

A hypothetical task: *In analysing the writing process, the research of both Bloggs (2006) and Smith and Jones (2008) has indicated the crucial role of metacognition. Discuss this claim in the light of your own experience as a first year university student.*

understanding your writing process

Here, the key WHAT words and therefore the key concepts to be researched are: *the writing process; the research of Bloggs (2006), Smith and Jones (2008); metacognition; your first year of university experience.*

key terms }

There may also be **evaluative terms** which you will need to consider, such as *more, most, major, all, some, few, least, better, best, almost, every*, etc.

In this example, the word *crucial* must be evaluated: is it crucial or just important, or not very important at all?

how is this information to be used?

Having researched the area, what are you expected to do with the information? HOW is it to be organised?

see: establishing a clear structure, Part 3 }

In the example above, you have been asked to discuss a claim in the light of your experience. This means that you have to briefly *describe* your relevant experience and *analyse* it to test if the claim is justified. You would need to *define* metacognition, *explain* the relevant parts of the researchers' work which would involve *analysing* the role of metacognition in the writing process, which would also need to be *described* and *explained* in this context.

Commonly, tasks can be organised as:

see: recognising types of essays, Part 3 }

» **descriptions** – what it is/was
» **explanations** – how a process occurs, how an event happened, often as a sequence of events
» **comparisons and contrasts** – how a number of ideas, processes, happenings are alike, or how they are different
» **discussions** of issues or problems, with analysis of possible solutions and implications.

patterns of organisation }

Frequently an assignment will ask you to use **several of these patterns of organisation**; such as *describe* and *explain* ; *compare* and *discuss* and so on. In analysing the task, you will need to decide on the principal purpose of the task, and to **balance** the various tasks. At university level, you are expected to move beyond description to more challenging tasks such as explanation, comparison or discussion. If you are asked to *outline* and *explain* or *discuss* within one assignment, remember to keep the description brief as the reader will probably be more interested in how you use the information to analyse and discuss it. A list of common task words can be found in the Appendix. You may wish to revisit the list of task words as the writing process proceeds and as you think further about what to include as your ideas evolve.

As mentioned earlier, consider your purpose and audience in writing this assignment. You may find that there are objectives for the subject listed in its outline which signal its expectations; for example an objective may be for students to develop critical thinking, or to observe a range of practices in a particular field. You should consider your task in the light of such objectives as it may help you to focus appropriately.

assessment criteria }

Assessment criteria, that is, a checklist of what is required in the assignment, may also be provided indicating how the marks will be apportioned. This enables you to check that you have not left out any part of the task, and that you have balanced the parts of the writing appropriately and strategically. For example, in one specific assignment, the Assessment Criteria indicated that *an outline* of an issue would be worth

10 marks and that *the discussion* of that issue with reference to at least three writers would be worth 30 marks. Clearly, you should give most of your attention to the discussion section of the assignment!

stage 2: researching & reading

remember purpose and audience

When you have analysed the wording of the task and feel clear about what is wanted, it is useful to brainstorm your first ideas as a guide to reading: what am I looking for? If you have no real idea yet about the topic, use the reading list as a starting point and later you can brainstorm from your notes.

For example, in planning the writing of this book, ideas were brainstormed. The list jumped from words like the *writing process* to *critical thinking, topic sentences* to *introduction* to *report-writing* to *referencing* and *apostrophes*, and so on. Clearly there was no easy connection between the ideas as they came; some represented a specific part of the process, others represented whole areas of academic writing. What is important is allowing your mind to toss the ideas up; you can impose a logical order on the list later.

At this early stage you may be gathering information in a variety of ways: searching online, reading a range of texts, interviewing, asking questions, working in the lab, viewing videos, and so on. You will need to plan how much time you can spend doing this. Conscientious students often need a reminder to halt the research stage in order to get started on the drafting. It is frequently easier to keep on reading and note-making than it is to start the writing, but there needs to be a point (marked in your diary) where you stop the research and start the writing. This does not mean that you will never need to go back to the research stage to fill a gap in your information or re-read an important text. However the writing process needs time if it is to work and do justice to the research you have done. Here are several tips that can help to make the research stage more efficient.

strategies

see: referencing, Part 7

» **Print or photocopy** whatever you need to read – hard copy is easier to work with as you can 'see' what you have, spread it out, shuffle it around. The problem with a computer screen is that it fragments the information to one or two screens at a time. Write notes on the texts as you work with them and if you own the book, write on it (it is only a tool, after all).

full bibliographic details?

» **Always copy down the full bibliographic details** of the text before you start. This ensures that you do not have to spend time later trying to find all the information. *RefWorks* and *EndNote* are useful bibliographic software (see Part 7) that will store the information for you. Always double-check as these programs are not infallible.

» **Always read pen-in-hand**, underlining or highlighting key words and main ideas on your printouts or photocopies.

margin notes in this book highlight information

» **Write margin notes**: key words or questions – this will help you find the information quickly when you need it.

» **Note** any ideas after reading – the sooner the better while your memory and impressions are fresh. For example, what were the main points/arguments? What evidence? Where does this text differ/agree with others? What ideas has it given you? Where to next?

Reading information texts requires different skills from other types of reading. If you browse through a text without underlining or jotting notes, you may only have a vague idea of key information and you will need to re-read to find what you want. Making margin notes is an efficient research method for assignment preparation.

stage 3: thinking & sorting to get to a plan

brainstorming – thinking it through

Brainstorm. Having read your research notes and referred back to the wording of the task so that it is fresh in your mind, jot down anything and everything you can think of that may be needed in the assignment on one piece of paper, like a shopping list. You will probably end up with a fairly jumbled list which captures the main points to be covered as well as particular examples, names, etc. Consider this list, adding and subtracting and looking for connections.

This stage can be quite short, for example a couple of days, or for a larger task, it might be useful to allow longer for thinking it through.

Try not to rush to the computer. When writing straight into the computer from notes it is easy to lose focus: a plan is essential. Allow time for the information you have been reading to filter through your mind. Often a new thought will come when you least expect it – be ready to jot down unexpected ideas. Students often report that this happens on the train, or when trying to sleep, or even in the shower! (A waterproof notebook!?) In thinking it through you may also decide **what** to include as you become clearer on the focus or scope of the task. Frequent brainstorming sessions – just getting ideas on a page – can be very helpful, leading to yet another brainstorm as you add and subtract from it. All of this may be messy but it is valuable processing.

A common problem with assignments which have been composed straight into the computer from research notes is that they are disjointed and lack flow: there is obviously no unifying structure. A cut-and-paste approach also leaves more chance for plagiarism as a source may be lost (see Part 7). Instead, aim to have a tentative plan emerge from this part of the process: a list of the main stages of the assignment in the order you might follow (a mindmap will help here: see below).

confused? }

Reflecting on the issues, and perhaps discussing them with other students or an adviser in an academic assistance centre are very valuable preparatory parts of the process. Refer back to the task frequently and if necessary ask your tutor for clarification. Feeling confused is a common experience as you think about the topic, particularly if you are considering contrasting views on an issue.

mindmapping – sorting into a plan

The aim is now to sort your material into a useful order that will help you cover all the important aspects of the task and begin to see how you might link and connect ideas and information. A useful sorting strategy at this stage is to sort your brainstorm into a mindmap, or flow chart:

1. write the key words of the task as a question or issue in a circle in the centre of a blank page
2. use branch lines to indicate items that stem from the central question (i.e. subsets of the issue)
3. add points to each subset from your research
4. keep sorting and adding evidence and examples; some may be grouped according to similarities while others may be contrary points
5. use different colours to distinguish branch lines when it starts to grow crowded.

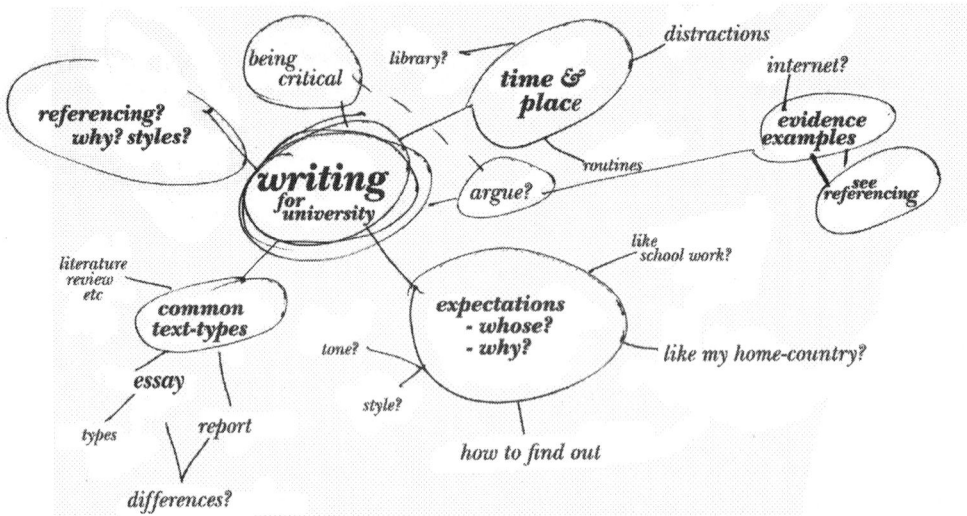

You are thus gaining a preliminary picture of the structure of your assignment and as you think it through, hopefully you will start to have an idea of what your theme in the assignment could be. This visual representation of the developing assignment has been found to help many writers to 'see' where they are going, suggesting it taps into right-brain processes.

Most writers readily recognise the messiness of these stages of the writing process. However, as you gain familiarity with your material you may find it becomes easier to start the actual writing.

drawing up a plan

Thinking it through, experimenting and mapping the assignment leads to the next stage of the process: **drawing up a plan, outline or list** of the order in which you will deal with the main points, that is, the sequence of the paragraphs of an essay or sections of a report. It may also show you where there are gaps, meaning that you have to go back to the research stage to find the missing information.

stage 4: drafting & editing

the drafting process

the stage of your text	purpose	audience
first draft → *free write* → *don't stop to polish* → *print out whole text* → *know that this is rough*	to clarify your ideas and structure	yourself
final draft → *edit for accuracy of content* → *check structure for logical development, signals and cohesion* → *proofread for spelling, grammar, referencing*	to communicate those ideas in a clear structure	assessor (lecturer/tutor)

understanding your writing process

Moving from your plan to adding details to each main stage of the writing will result in a rough early draft. Knowing that you have time to add to and amend this draft is important, as at this stage you are not preparing the version that someone else will read. The purpose of this draft is to clarify **your** ideas, and the audience at this stage is **yourself**. You may not yet even have a clear idea of your point of view on an issue. Frequently, by the conclusion of this first draft a theme emerges – **the light comes on**! – that is, you begin to have your thesis or point of view about the topic.

free write

It is often a useful strategy to **free write** this first draft: just to write to see how the assignment develops. At this stage, do not be concerned about 'sounding' academic: a first draft may be easier if you write informally, perhaps as you speak. The main aim is to get the ideas down on paper – you can change the tone and style at a later stage. Composing on a computer fragments the text because you only see parts, not the whole, so it is important to **print out the entire text**. Otherwise, you may be tempted to revise and refine one paragraph or part, which can be very distracting before the whole text is complete. The assignment may then become more an awkward cut-and-paste exercise, rather than a fluent text. Free write to the end, print out and read through with a **pen-in-hand** to correct and amend the text. This is when you begin to edit and proofread the assignment. It is useful to understand that writing often develops from the first draft as a clarifying process, to enable you to 'get a handle' on the task, into a final polished text that others can read without losing their way.

pen-in-hand

the editing process

» **Refer back** to the wording of the task/question to check that each paragraph is relevant and adds something to the answer. It is common in first-draft writing to go off on a tangent, so it is important to test each paragraph for relevance by asking: how does this paragraph contribute to answering the task? Read back through your notes to check that you have not neglected an area. **Check** that any generalisation or assertion that you have made is supported.

don't pad!
see: word count, Part 7

» **Add and delete**. You may need to add examples to explanations and elaborate to ensure that your meaning is clear. Do not be tempted to add extra words in order to meet the word count! If you do not have enough to meet the minimum word count, explore further in your reading and re-visit your lecture notes in case you have overlooked some areas of the task. Remember, each paragraph must be relevant.

see: paragraphing, Part 7

see: paragraph test

On the other hand, if your word count is over the maximum specified, check for repetition and redundancy. Again, ask if each paragraph has a place in answering the task and is justified in being there: does it pass the 'paragraph test'? (See below.)

Your draft is moving closer to being the final product as you edit and proofread for relevance and logical development; moving text about, adding or deleting, expanding or tightening the information or argument. It is useful now to leave this nearly-final draft for a day, or longer if possible, so that when you return to it, you may notice any problems – you will have distanced yourself from the text and will read it more as the intelligent stranger!

the intelligent stranger: get feedback

When you are reasonably satisfied that the assignment has a structure and a sequence of paragraphs that makes sense, it is useful to get some feedback, maybe from another student, or a tutor who may agree to read a draft, or from an academic writing adviser. The assignment is moving now towards its final version, to be read by your lecturer or tutor.

stage 5: polishing & proofreading

You can see that as you edit and proofread you are moving towards a final polishing of the text. Check now at the sentence level for spelling and grammar, as errors are frequently very irritating to the reader (the assessor, or an employer). You will notice from time to time in the media that letters and articles are written proclaiming a decline in literacy – and most of the attention is focussed on writers' spelling and grammar, or the incorrect use of a word because they are so noticeable, rather than issues of clear argumentation or the use of evidence.

see Part 8

If you have carefully checked your text (perhaps by reading it aloud) you should be able to correct such errors. Using a computer may mean that a typing error escapes your attention, particularly if the automatic spellchecker recognises it as a correctly-spelled word (for example, there is a big difference between *lose* and *loose*). You also need to be aware that most computers give American spelling rather than Australian/British (for example, *color* or *colour*? *recognise* or *recognize*?). Common grammatical errors are discussed later (see Part 8), but if you have concerns about your grammatical understanding, consider using a grammar textbook or attending a grammar course. Your aim should be to understand what is troubling you so that you do not have to rely on someone else proofreading your writing each time. However, in the first instance, it may be very useful to consult an academic adviser.

see: demons! Part 8

see Part 7

At this stage of the writing process you should carefully check your in-text citations and reference list for consistency and accuracy. In some faculties you may lose marks for inaccurate or inconsistent referencing.

what does my faculty expect?

Check also the visual presentation of your assignment and ensure that you follow any instructions. Double spacing between lines and wide margins are usually expected to allow comments to be written. Extra space between paragraphs with no indentation is usually preferred. Most lecturers do not want an assignment where every page is in a plastic sleeve.

paragraphing

a paragraph is a chunk of meaning

It may be helpful to think of constructing an assignment at the planning and drafting stages in terms of paragraphs, rather than sentences (the microview) or the essay or report itself (the macroview).

the paragraph is the building block

A paragraph is conventionally defined as a number of sentences about one main point; when the writer gets to the next main point or step, a new paragraph is needed. Imagine reading a novel or newspaper without paragraphing. You would feel quite frustrated as you tried to make sense of it. The paragraph is a convention of writing that we learn from a very early age and that we come to expect without really thinking about it. However, when writing a university assignment, you need to be very conscious of how your paragraphs are working to communicate your understanding and information.

It is worth spending time on this matter of construction by paragraphs, for if you analyse an 'easy-to-read' text that seems to 'flow', you will find that the writer has a clear structure which you have been able to follow. This is often because the writer has used topic sentences and signal words to highlight the purpose and relevance of a particular paragraph to the overall text. In notemaking, recognising topic sentences gives you key words, and the overall list of these key words can be seen to be an outline or skeleton of the text. In your writing, start with a skeleton of key words (your plan) and build paragraphs from the key words, using topic sentences. As you add substance to your plan and the assignment grows, topic sentences and signals should make the structure explicit and logical to the reader.

The paragraph test: when you are proofreading for relevance, ask yourself if each paragraph passes the 'paragraph test', that is, ask what this paragraph contributes to the whole text. Can you justify its existence? Is it adding to the information or giving a contrasting point of view? Is it establishing the first step in the development of the topic or is it explaining a cause for an occurrence?
Then test if you have made this explicit in the first sentence of the paragraph so that the reader is in no doubt about its relevance. Writing a topic sentence which explicitly links this paragraph to the argument or information of the task is a sure way to ensure its relevance. If you cannot tie the paragraph into the task in this way, even though you may have worked hard to construct it, throw it out! Topic sentences and signal words are explained below.

topic sentences and signal words

The topic sentence encapsulates a paragraph, and is usually most effective as the first sentence in that paragraph. Just as the introduction to an essay or report provides the reader with an overview of what to expect, so the first sentence of a paragraph can perform the same function. This first sentence also should provide a connection to the previous paragraph by signalling if the information to follow is more of the same (*similarly ... ; another feature ... ; in addition ... ; furthermore ...*) or if the writer is about to contrast new information with that previously given (*however ... ; a contrasting view ... ; unlike ...*). The signalling word or words in the topic sentence may also indicate that this paragraph provides the next point or stage of an explanation or process (*The first main stage ... ; The next significant feature ... ; The final ... ; Consequently ...*)

see: cohesion

In a first draft, writers frequently are more concerned with the content of their argument or explanation, and rightly so, but in subsequent drafts, you need to make that content clear for your reader. By writing topic sentences which make it explicit how and why the paragraph has been

reader-friendly texts! } written, the writer provides a cohesive structure that is easy to follow. Paragraphs without topic sentences make more demands on the reader who has to work out why this particular paragraph has been included, perhaps forcing them to pause in the reading and go back to previous paragraphs in order to make a connection. You want the reader to go forwards, with a sense of the material unfolding, not to hesitate and go back and forth through the text!

In report writing, the use of headings and subheadings achieves a similar effect, providing the key words for that section of the text and enabling the reader to predict the structure. Topic sentences in first paragraphs are still helpful to the reader: use the key words from the heading or the task to provide a link with what is to follow. (See Part 4 for details and examples.)

In constructing paragraphs, it is often useful to provide a restatement sentence, that is, a summary sentence to close the paragraph, which also provides a hook for the next paragraph to latch onto. The summary sentence ensures that after reading a lot of details, examples or evidence in the paragraph, the reader is reminded of the main idea, which then links the paragraph to the overall task or question.

an example } Here is an example of a paragraph using an opening topic sentence, signal words and a restatement sentence, each of which is underlined.

> *Writing an assignment for academic purposes may be a difficult process for the beginning writer, who needs to understand it is not a single task. As well as* understanding how to interpret what is required in the assignment, the student needs to have efficient research and planning strategies. It *also* helps to realise that it is very useful to write several drafts, rather than attempting to write the final version in one step. *Another* important strategy is managing time, so that there is sufficient time for reflection and getting feedback. *In this way* the final version will have advanced from the initial ideas to an edited and more polished version. *Understanding how to manage the parts of the process is therefore an important part of assignment writing.*

cohesion

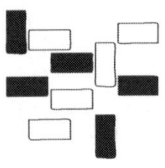

The effect of topic sentences and signal words is called cohesion, which has been considerably researched in language and linguistic studies. For your purposes, this notion can be simply explained by viewing a text as a construction where each paragraph is pictured as a building block that leads the reader, step by step towards your final point, or conclusion. The 'glue' holding the construction together in this metaphor is the topic sentence, with signal words providing explicit links.

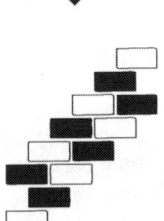

Many assignments resemble a random pile of blocks, that is, paragraphs on the page which have no obvious connection. If there is no recognisable structure or organisation, the reader will be asking: why are the paragraphs assembled in this particular order? Is the first paragraph there because it is the most important point, or is it background information that is necessary before other information can be explained?

The reader is then really doing the writer's job in trying to sort through the blocks to build connections. Although the paragraphs may be full of relevant information, if they are not glued together, they are not part of an overall construction. There is a considerable risk that the reader will become confused and lost in the argument and information. Therefore there needs to be a logical development, a connection from one block to the next that will make sense to the reader. Topic sentences and signal words provide this cohesion and hold the text together. Furthermore, as many assignment topics encourage argument and a point of view, each student's construction of an assignment may be different. This makes it even more important to signal your particular argument or explanation quite explicitly.

It is useful **to plan** the essay or report by headings or a list of key words so that you can see how one point will lead to the next, as explained in *sorting into a plan* (above). This is why it is suggested that you spend some time thinking through connections and how your argument or explanation will develop. The sorting and ordering process may take you in different directions as you think it through; it is better to spend time establishing the direction of your writing at this stage than to hand in an unconnected 'draft' or to rush the organisation of the material at the end. It is easier to change a plan than to change an essay!

exam essays

Much of the above advice is useful when preparing to write an essay in exam conditions, under time pressure. The important stages should not be neglected as you want to get the best result from the limited writing time.

Firstly be sure to read through the entire exam paper before starting to write an essay. Check the mark allocation; if each essay attracts the same number of marks, try to allocate your time evenly. If one question is worth more, of course give it more time. If you have not prepared for a question, try to write something rather than nothing; then give extra time to the other questions to try to recoup the marks. Use the reverse side of the exam pad for ideas and be sure to draw a line through your jottings afterwards so that they are not confused with your essay.

researching

pen-in-hand

This is your preparation before the exam, perhaps memorising information (dates, terms, definitions etc.). **Read pen-in-hand** over lecture notes as well as your textbooks to be sure of areas that have been emphasised in class. If the library or the faculty website has copies of past exam papers, practise writing essays to a time limit so that you practise the techniques suggested below and also become familiar with the topics.

interpreting the task

This is a key step in writing a relevant essay. Whether there are set questions or a choice from a range of topics, spend time carefully reading each task, paying particular attention to the **key content words** (what information or concepts are to be written about?); to any **evaluative terms** (such as *more, most, every*), and to the **task words** (such as *explain, discuss, compare*). Decide the balance of these tasks: how much of the essay (and therefore time) should you spend on each part?

thinking and sorting to get a plan

Even though you may feel pressured to begin writing as quickly as possible, a few minutes spent **brainstorming** from your memory will be very useful (perhaps allow five minutes of a 40 minute task). Jot down anything you have memorised – words and phrases, definitions, dates or figures as they come to mind – to free your brain to concentrate on the task. Know that your memory will probably not be systematic so give it a chance to come up with what you have learnt. Then **sort through** to decide the most relevant order or sequence in which to use these ideas or facts. This becomes a rough plan.

plan by key words which become topic sentences

It is much better to rough this out **before writing** the essay than to write the essay as ideas come to you, which may be an erratic process. If you can think it through as you draw up a plan, you can subsequently concentrate more on the writing and not have to stop and start while waiting for the next idea. Your text will then have more coherence as you argue or explain.

drafting, editing, polishing and proofreading

These processes have to happen almost simultaneously. This is why it is better to have a plan to work from as you write so that you can think about writing a topic sentence to link each paragraph to the task, and incorporate evidence and examples for each main point. When you have finished, read over and check for the development of argument or steps in an explanation and so on, as well as grammar, spelling and punctuation.

The only consolation about the difficulty of doing so much in what is really a first draft piece of writing is that everyone doing the exam is in the same situation. Given more time, probably everybody could write a better essay. It is important that you recognise what the essay task is asking for and that you demonstrate how much you know about the topic. Topic sentences will help to keep you, and the reader, on the task. However, no amount of clever writing techniques will compensate for lack of knowledge so make sure that you are prepared!

choosing the text type – essay or report?

see Part 3 and Part 4

The general terms used to describe academic assignments are usually the essay and the report. Within each of these general terms there are subsets.

In the choice of a text type, there are three important aspects to consider:
» its purpose and audience
» the steps or stages that are conventionally expected for that particular type of text. If you are unsure, check your Faculty Referencing Guidelines, or ask.
» the language features conventionally expected for that particular type of text; for example, how personal or impersonal is it expected to be?

Usually, the lecturer will specify the type of text required and will provide instructions and sometimes guidelines for the writing. However, in tasks such as learning contracts or a major study, the student, in consultation with the lecturer, may select a topic of interest to research and so may have a choice about the type of text that will be written; for example, an argumentative essay or an information report. In this case, select the text type that will help you to organise your material, and that will be easy to follow.

the essay:

the report:

There are significant differences in how the material is presented in an essay and a report but remember also that this may vary depending on a particular lecturer's expectations. The main difference is that an essay usually is expected to be a piece of writing where ideas and information flow from one paragraph to the next. Topic sentences and signal words serve the purpose of making the connections. It is also expected that evidence and examples are integrated into the text in a fluent manner, and that the writer takes the reader on a journey that develops logically towards the conclusion. It would be difficult for a reader to read just a paragraph of an essay without the context provided by the other paragraphs. For example, if you have researched an issue and are presenting your point of view based on logical reasoning and evidence, an essay that flows cohesively would be suitable. It may sometimes be acceptable to use headings to add organisation to an essay but this will depend on your tutor or lecturer, whom you should consult to be sure. Dot points or numbered points are rarely acceptable.

In a report, however, each section is clearly labelled and self-contained so that the reader can choose to read a particular section, and this text type may be appropriate if you have a lot of information to present. In some sections, dot points or numbered points may be the best means of listing or sequencing information. Headings and subheadings provide the reader with a clear map through the text, matching the table of contents which gives an overview of the whole text. Topic sentences at the beginning of paragraphs are used to pick up the key words from headings or subheadings so that although the text may seem sectioned into separate pieces, it nevertheless is connected and logical.

last draft checklist

Check the task instructions to be sure of the following:

→ What does the reader need to know? ≈ have I provided the necessary background to the issues?
→ What needs to be explained? ≈ have I defined the key terms of the task?
→ Is my text logically structured? ≈ have I used explicit topic sentences and signal words to direct the reader through my text?
→ Is the tone pitched at the expected level for this particular task? ≈ have I analysed the wording of the question to see if I am invited to be a participant or is the focus on the issue? (See Part 5.)
→ Have I made it clear what sources I have relied on? ≈ have I fully acknowledged each source of information/evidence? (See Part 7.)
→ Have I proofread thoroughly? (See Part 8.)

3.

academic writing is . . .
writing the essay

establishing a clear structure:
  the introduction
  the body
  the conclusion

writing the body of the essay by recognising purpose
  the expository essay: the essay that informs
  » *description*
  » *explanation*
  » *comparison-contrast*
  the discussion essay: the essay that argues & evaluates
  » *argument, analysis & critical analysis, critical evaluation*

model discussion essay

checklist

establishing a clear structure

Traditional essay genres at this time remain the conventional means of much student assessment, although in the future, technological advances may mean innovative alternatives, such as interactive digital and multimodal texts combining words, images and even sounds. In the present context it is important that the beginning writer develops a flexible repertoire of writing skills, starting with the essay.

There are different types of essays for different purposes, but all have three basic parts: an introduction, a body and a conclusion. The initial and final paragraphs can be viewed as rhetorical or stylistic devices, that is, like the first and last speaker in a debate: the introduction sets the stage and provides the audience with an expectation of the text that follows, while the conclusion announces the end of the text and ties the threads of the body together. The evidence of your research will be contained in the body of the essay and this will be where most of the marks for the assignment are earned through your descriptions, explanations, comparisons, arguments, evidence and examples. However, it is also important to realise that this work needs to be placed in a context where it makes sense for the reader, connecting your scholarly work to the task you were given.

Preview
↓
Body
↓
Review

It is usually the function of the introduction to establish that context, and the function of the conclusion to reiterate the connection between your assignment and the task. All three parts are therefore interrelated and are expected in any assignment.

the introduction:

"tell them what you're going to tell them"

The first paragraph of an assignment has particular purposes. It is not enough merely to repeat the wording of the task: the reader in this academic culture expects to be able to predict how the text will develop. The introduction thus identifies the task being addressed, provides some context for the writing and previews the thesis statement or point of view of the writer. Remember that academic writing usually follows the convention of previewing the whole before embarking on the parts. For example, a task may instruct:

> *Discuss the importance of writing competence in students' success at university.*

Like the old adage:
— *Tell them what you're going to tell them.*
— *Tell them.*
— *Tell them what you've told them!*

the structure of an introduction: plan by sentences

» it makes a general statement about the issue or area under discussion.
  For example: *More students are attending university than ever before ... and it is important to investigate the factors that contribute to their success.*

» it gives a preview of the main structure of the assignment.
  For example: *In evaluating several significant studies in this area, it is clear that key factors relate to student motivation, the perceived relevance of a course of study and less clearly defined social and cultural factors.*

» it may mention the scope or limitation of the assignment.
  For example: *... in Australia today*

In this context, a thesis is your proposition to be argued/explained; not to be confused with a research-based dissertation.

» it states the writer's thesis. It is definitely useful to use the **key terms** of the task to signify the focus of the assignment, and if this can be combined with a statement about the writer's point of view (frequently called a **thesis**), the reader will be in no doubt about the direction of the assignment.

For example: *If success is taken to be students' completion of their degree course in the minimum time without failed subjects, it is important to analyse the factors that enable them to pass exams and assignments. This then emphasises the need to ensure competence in writing as a key component of success.*

The full example of an introduction as planned above:

More students are attending university in Australia today than ever before, and it is important to investigate the factors that contribute to their success. In evaluating several significant studies in this area, it is clear that key factors relate to student motivation, the perceived relevance of a course of study and less clearly defined social and cultural factors. If success is taken to be students' completion of their degree course in the minimum time without failed subjects, it is important to analyse the factors that enable them to pass exams and assignments. This then emphasises the need to ensure competence in writing as a key component of success.

In light of what has been said earlier about the writing process and the suggestion that the first draft should be a free-write, it follows that often a writer may not be really clear about the thesis at this stage. Writing is a very useful clarifying process and often you can explore what you think and where the evidence leads you **by writing**. Therefore, many writers find that they write their introduction at a later stage, when they are clearer about their message. Because the introduction has a rhetorical function (much like setting a stage), it can be written last with attention to making it fit the expectations outlined above. In practical terms this often means re-writing the conclusion (where your writing and thinking has led you) and framing it as an introduction (where you preview that direction).

Some assignments require you to write an abstract, described in Part 6, which is not the same as an introduction.

the body:

"tell them"

The body of the essay is where the evidence of your research and thinking are assembled and here you will be assessed on the development and relevance of your information and any discussion based on that information, supported by your research which should be carefully acknowledged.

The body of an essay is where you show your hard work in gathering and using information and it is here that the bulk of the marks usually lie. Several strands of information or discussion may be developed and interwoven as the text progresses.

the structure of the body: plan by paragraphs

see: paragraphing

As the way that you structure the body of your assignment will depend on its purpose, that is, the type of text it is. **Details for specific structures for different types of essays are suggested in the next section,** *recognising types of essays.*

the conclusion:

"tell them what you've told them"

Just as the introduction is a rhetorical device, providing a **preview**, so too the conclusion needs to meet several expectations. It is a **review** of the text.

the structure of a conclusion: plan by sentences

» it sums up the arguments of the whole text (drawing together the main strands).
For example: *The main focus for researchers ... on such areas ... has shown the complexity of the issues ... A principal factor ... shown to be their writing competence ... more research should be directed ...*

» it makes reference to the key terms of the task (reminding the reader of how the text started).
For example: *... factors affecting student success at university ... enabling students to pass exams and assignments ...*

» it re-iterates and confirms the main thesis (connecting the end of the writing with the beginning).
For example: *A principal factor that emerges from recent research examining students' ability to pass exams and assignments, has been shown to be their writing competence ...*

» it may suggest recommendations or indicate the significance or implications that follow from the conclusion.
For example: *... and it is to this area that more research should be directed in the current Australian context.*

The full example of a conclusion as planned above:
The main focus for researchers in several significant studies into the factors affecting student success at university has so far been on such areas as student motivation and how relevant a course of study is seen to be. There has also been some research into social and cultural factors which has shown the complexity of the issues, needing more research for clarification. A principal factor that emerges from recent research examining students' ability to pass exams and assignments has been shown to be their writing competence, and it is to this area that more research should be directed.

An essential proofreading step is to read your introduction and conclusion together to ensure that you have not added to, or changed, your argument in the course of writing the body, and in fact that you have done what you set out to do. There should be no new information in the conclusion. If you find you have added something not mentioned before, check that it is relevant and if so, include it as a paragraph in the body of your text. If during the body you have changed your argument, or gone off on a tangent, it is essential to make sure either that the introduction reflects all the main directions of the argument or information, or that you discard the pieces that do not fit with your overview. Try the 'paragraph test' (see Part 2) and examine each paragraph to justify its existence in the assignment. Remember cohesion, that is, there should be a predictable link from one paragraph to the next which can be achieved using signal words (see *topic sentences* and *signal words* below).

writing the body of the essay by recognising purpose

Typically, tasks may be analysed to determine their essential purpose, and a list of the main structures or patterns of organisation follows.

types of essays

There are two main types of essay for different purposes:
1. the essay that informs (an expository or explanatory essay)
2. the essay that argues (a discussion or critical analysis or evaluation).

As has been previously stated, many assignments will require you to integrate several tasks. However, for clarity each particular structure is explained separately below. It is followed by a list of typical instructions for the assignment to enable you to recognise the structure that is required, with suggestions for planning, and explicit examples. Effective signal words for cohesion, and notes on appropriate language choices (i.e. the tense and personal pronouns to use) then follow.

the expository essay: the essay that informs

The basic aim of an expository essay is to inform and explain a process, an event or series of events. The way that you structure your essay should reflect what you think is the over-riding purpose of the task which may be:
» a description
» an explanation
» a comparison-contrast.

a description:

where the purpose is to provide information or to tell about something, usually in a logical order (often in a time sequence: for example, a history topic, or a description of a scientific process). A description may be necessary to set a context before you proceed to an explanation, comparison or discussion.

typical instructions for a description may be

describe	tell about features, factors, qualities
outline	list the main or general points
identify	select and list the main features, factors
indicate	point out and list the main features, factors
enumerate	specify and list the main features (one by one)
define	set out the meaning (of a term, word); describe (and sometimes explain)
illustrate	make clear, give examples
summarise	give a succinct description
review	in the sense of giving a list, an overview

Or the task may be framed as
write about ... or as a question: *what are/were the main factors in ... ?*
what are/were the main features/aspects of ... ?

planning to write a description:
using brainstorms > mindmaps > lists

Consider your reader. What terms should be defined at the beginning to make your understanding clear? What information does the reader need at the beginning of the description: where is the logical starting point?

You may wish to begin with the most important event or factor, or you may need to work chronologically through a series of facts or ideas.

Here is a simple example. The task is to describe the chair you are sitting on. Where would you start? Brainstorm all its features (office chair, blue fabric, swivels, movable back, goes up and down, etc.). Now make a mind map where you group the features of the chair together (its uses; the materials of its construction; its special features, etc.) and decide on a logical order to present to someone else. You may wish to describe its overall usefulness (the 'big picture') before moving to its appearance (*This is a specifically designed office chair*... then the details) or you may think it more effective to begin with a detailed picture and conclude with a summary about its overall worth as an item of furniture. List the sequence of sentences (and for an assignment, a list of paragraphs) as the basis for your plan. The description that emerges then has a logical structure that the reader can easily follow, rather than the random order of features that were first thought of.

signals to use in your topic sentence that help to link your material in a description include:

> *An important factor ... In addition ... Furthermore ... Moreover ... Another feature of ... An additional aspect ... As well as ... further reasons/aspects ...*

If you are sequencing your description, some signals are:
> *Firstly ... in the beginning ... then ... the next main ... later ... when ... while ... eventually ... lastly ... finally ... the concluding step ...*

tense and pronoun choice

Language choices: use the past tense to describe events that are over, and third person pronouns to keep an impersonal tone.

an explanation:

chain of events

where the purpose is to explain the relationship between events or ideas in a cause and effect sequence, telling what happened (or happens) and why, and what the outcomes were (or are); or to give reasons for a circumstance and the results of it. An explanation may be needed so that you can proceed to more analytical writing, such as a comparison or discussion.

typical instructions for an explanation may be

explain	give reasons for, clarify
account for	give reasons for, explain
discuss	in the sense of, account for
give a rationale for	give reasons, explain why
justify	give reasons

Or the task may be framed as
> *how does/did ... ; why do/did ... ; give reasons for ... ; explain why ... ; show how x leads to y ...*

planning to write an explanation:
using cause > effect (or outcome < reason) chains

It is important that you organise your explanation so that it makes sense to the reader, that is, what needs to be explained first? What background context (possibly a description) is needed to set the scene? It may be helpful to sort your material into cause and effect diagrams.

One event may have several causes so that you need to make this clear in your signalling (*the main cause ... ; the initial cause ...*) and similarly, there

may be more than one outcome or effect, some of which may be *immediate effects* while others may be *long-term outcomes*. To make it more complicated, an outcome of an event or idea may then become the cause of the next significant happening. In the planning stages it may be easier to make a graphical 'cause and effect chain' so that you can more easily see the development to be explained, for example in this simple narrative of events:
> *the neighbour's baby cried all night > I had no sleep > I was late for the exam > I made many mistakes > I failed the paper.*

chronological: describing events as they happen
hindsight: looking back at the events from a given point

You can easily see the chain of cause and effect, but it is important to realise that there would be reasons for the baby crying all night, further back in time, and there would be outcomes beyond failing the exam, further into the future. Your assignment would need to make the context clear (*I live in a large inner city apartment block*) and perhaps indicate the possible implications for the future (*In the future I will schedule my exam revision well in advance*) and the scope or limitations of your current explanation in the broader context (*Of course there are other reasons for my lack of preparation, but the most immediate cause of my poor performance was lack of sleep the night before the exam*).

Arrange your explanation in a logical order so that the focus is on your main point, in this example, failing the exam. This may not be the chronological order of events as often interest lies in outcomes, and explanations are given with hindsight. A simple chain of events in sequence/chronological order can be re-arranged to explain an outcome. For example:

> *Leaving my exam preparation until the last minute <u>means</u> that unexpected circumstances <u>have resulted</u> in disaster! I <u>have just received</u> my exam results in the mail and I <u>have failed</u> a key subject. I <u>may have to repeat</u> the subject or leave university. This <u>means</u> I <u>will not get</u> the job I <u>want</u> because I <u>failed</u> the exam paper. The reason for this <u>was</u> that on the night before the exam, the neighbour's baby <u>cried</u> all night. As a result I <u>had</u> no sleep and I <u>was</u> late for the exam and this <u>caused</u> me to make many mistakes.*

This re-arrangement starts with **an overall cause-effect statement (topic sentence)**: *Leaving my exam preparation until the last minute means that unexpected circumstances have resulted in disaster!* (because)
context: (where, when, what is happening): *I have just received my exam results in the mail and I have failed a key subject.* (so)
long-term effects: *I may have to repeat the subject or leave university and I will not get the job I wanted.* (because)
more immediate effect: *I failed the exam paper.* (because)
first cause in sequence chain: *on the night before the exam, the neighbour's baby <u>cried</u> all night.* (so)
next: *I <u>had</u> no sleep.* (so)
next: *I <u>was</u> late for the exam.* (so)
next: *<u>caused</u> me to make many mistakes.*

In this sad example, obviously the writer has over-simplified the causes of the disaster and should analyse at more depth! Similarly, there would be other outcomes. Your writing tasks are more complex than this example; nevertheless, it shows that often an explanation begins by providing a context for the explanation and focuses on outcomes, before giving the reasons to explain the events. The example also shows that it is often significant in your analysis to differentiate between immediate and long-term causes and effects.

signals to use in your topic sentence that help to link your material in an explanation include:
The main reason/cause ... ; as a result/outcome/effect ... ; as a consequence ... ; consequently, therefore, because, if, unless, this is why ... ; so that, so ...

tense and pronoun choice

Language choices: use past tense if the events are over, but use the 'timeless' present tense to comment on those events. In the example above, notice how the verbs (underlined) change tense in this way (e.g. *means* – present; *cried* – past). In this example first person pronouns have been used for a reflection; more often an academic explanation would be in third person.

a comparison – contrast:

where the purpose is to show similarities and/or differences between events, ideas, practices, etc. This may also be needed before proceeding to an analysis, explanation or discussion.

typical instructions for a comparison-contrast may be
compare show the similarities and differences
contrast emphasise the differences between

The task may be framed as a question:
How does Theory X differ from Theory Y? or How does Bloggs' theory of ... help you to understand your recent experiences in the workplace?

This is a hidden comparison where you are really comparing the explanation given in Bloggs' theory to your experiences to decide if it adequately accounts for what happened.

the hidden comparison

Similarly, there is a hidden comparison in a task which asks you to discuss the advantages and disadvantages of something. For example:
Discuss the advantages and disadvantages to the economy of the current government's policy on higher education. Essentially, you are comparing the positive features with the negative features of the policy to enable you to come to a conclusion.

Less obvious signals for writing a comparison-contrast are words such as *more, most,* or *less, least.* The suffix (or ending on a word) that indicates a comparison (*-er, -est*) also signals that you are expected to do more than describe. For example, an assignment may ask you to discuss a proposition such as:
Students write <u>better</u> essays when they are aware of the importance of structure and signals. Discuss.

This task implies a comparison of the writing of those who know about structure and those who do not, or a before-and-after comparison of students' writing with regard to the claim. Evaluate the claim from evidence. You can see how this type of task requires you to do several things: *compare, explain* and *evaluate*. You also need a definition of *better* – what makes an essay better, and in whose view? Similarly there is a comparison implied in the following assignment task:
Discuss the claim that student writers' main difficulty in writing assignments relates to time management.

Here you would need to compare all the difficulties students may have to evaluate whether time management is the main one. Again, the instruction to *discuss* involves a comparison of ideas and information.

planning to write a comparison-contrast: using a comparison grid

After your reading, brainstorm the areas you can think of to compare and/or contrast. It is then useful to plot these factors in a comparison grid (see below) or spreadsheet.

This is the sort of thinking consumers often do when comparing products, whether it is breakfast cereal or a new car, where a list of for-and-against factors assists the analysis process. In the academic context it becomes very useful to sift your research in the same way.

For example, a simplified task is to compare three city universities. Brainstorm the areas that need to be compared such as courses offered, location, social activities, or cost, and check the wording of the assignment task and your lecture notes for areas of emphasis. Build up a list of features for the first column, adding or eliminating features as you think it through. Brief notes from your research in each column provide the evidence for the body of the assignment (facts, figures, opinions from researchers etc.). Areas of similarity and difference can then become a guide to paragraph planning as you arrange these features into a sequence for writing the assignment.

features for comparison	University A	University B	University C
1. courses offered			
2. location			
3. social activities			
4. cost			
5. etc.			

This sorting enables you to see two aspects clearly:
» **reading down** a column gives you a description of one item or idea
» **reading along** the row gives you a comparison across all items or ideas regarding one particular feature.

If you were to write an essay based on the above information, your introduction would preview your main finding (that is, the preferred university) and the body would then systematically explore the comparison based on each feature in turn, paragraph by paragraph. You may decide that one feature (for example, the cost) is more important than others and so you would prioritise this in the body of the essay. Your conclusion would sum up:

> ... based on research of several important features, the most suitable choice of university would be ...

The grid, or organiser thus provides a useful plan for the writing.

This of course is a simplified example for reasons of space. The graphic organiser can be applied to quite complex comparisons. For example, you could compare a collection of poems by one poet to look for similar themes, uses of language and imagery. You could compare the policies of different political parties in a particular area to examine where ideas coincide and where there are significant contrasts.

signals to use in your topic sentence that help to link your material in a comparison-contrast include:
On the one hand ... ; on the other ... ; however/ yet/ but/ though/ despite ... ; either ... ; or ... ; In comparison ... ; In contrast ... ; On the contrary ...

However is a significant signal in a comparison: it enables you to describe and explain one aspect of the subject (for example, the advantages of something) and then to move across to describe and explain the other side (the disadvantages), which is essentially a comparison of two or more views of an issue. Without a clear signal between opposing ideas, your text may appear confused and muddled to the reader and it may seem that you have changed direction without explanation, or that you are leaving it to the reader to imply conclusions. If you feel unsure about your viewpoint, more thinking is required and a free-write or conversation with other students may help to sort it out.

see: model discussion essay, for a comparison table that provides evidence for an argument

Language choices: use the present tense to indicate that the comparison is on-going, rather than completed (e.g. *The most suitable choice is ...* not *The most suitable choice was ...*). Be wary of superlatives such as *best* or *worst* unless you really have exhaustive evidence. How is *best* to be defined? Try more informative words that are appropriate and specific to the context, such as *more effective in ... , more useful to ... , more relevant to ...* and have evidence in support. Use the impersonal third person pronoun unless your own views have been invited in the task.

the discussion essay: the essay that argues & evaluates

In writing a discussion essay, you will be interpreting information (or data) and/or ideas and frequently evaluating or making judgements about the worth (or usefulness, relevance, appropriateness and so on) of that information and/or ideas, often by comparisons and contrasts of points of view. Your own point of view, or thesis, will depend on all these processes of comparison, analysis, synthesis and evaluation.

see Part 7: academic debate vs everyday argument

argument
To *argue* in the academic sense means to put forward a point of view on an issue, supported by logical reasoning and evidence. To do this, you may have to balance contrasting views, reasoning and evidence. In this sense it is similar to debating a subject.

In doing so, you are sometimes asked to give a **critical** analysis or to critically evaluate other points of view, research or explanations. Before describing strategies for doing this, it is important for you to be clear about your purpose, and about what is expected when these terms are used.

see also Part 1: being critical

analysis and critical analysis
In analysing an issue, you need to examine the essential features of a point of view, an explanation, theory, or an experience, therefore ask some or all of these questions:
» What is the context of this issue? (where and when?)
» What is the main point or thesis? (what?)
» Who is making this assertion? What interests does this view represent? Are there gaps or silences – how are contrasting views represented, if at all? (who?)
» What evidence or argument is used to support this view? (how?)

» How is this writer presenting this view or experience: in what terms, from what perspective? with what sort of language – persuasive, argumentative, authoritative? (how?)
» Why is this point of view being put forward? (why?)
» What does this writer want me, the reader, to do – to agree? take action? (so what?)

It is usually clear when you read political or advertising material that the writer wants you to vote a certain way, or buy a certain product. In academic argument, writers may also be persuading you that their interpretation of circumstances is the logical or 'natural' or 'universal' way to view them. You can critique the writer's position by asking the questions above, and also by making an alternative reading of the argument (that is, put yourself in the 'alternate' reader's position). Writers frequently assume that the reader shares their same values, but these assumptions may become more transparent, and therefore open to criticism, when viewed from a different perspective. The critical reader is one who asks questions and looks for gaps or limitations in an argument, asking where this argument may lead, what or who may have been left out, and perhaps who gains and who loses from possible outcomes.

As you consider contentions from different viewpoints you can see a discussion emerging, one that will need evidence from research and theories for support. In developing a thesis, or point of view, you will need to draw on evidence that supports your view but will also need to refer to contrary evidence that does not agree, showing the gaps or limitations. Frequently students ask if they should refer to an opposing viewpoint, or just ignore it. The answer has to be that you demonstrate your knowledge of the issue with reference to the contrasting points of view, explaining the limitations and arguing for your point of view. If you do not mention that there are different perspectives, you are not dealing with them and therefore you are giving an unbalanced argument. It also may look like you have not read widely enough to know that conflicting views exist!

critical evaluation

A step further on from a critical analysis is to ask questions about the value or worth of what you have found from your analysis. How useful or valuable is the idea or practice – to whom, where and when? What is its importance, significance and relevance? What implications are there? What is needed next? For example, if your task was to *critically evaluate Bloggs' theories on effective writing*, you would need to establish the context of the issues, then move from a *description* and *explanation* of these theories to an *analysis* of each part of the theories and finally give an *evaluation* of their significance. This might also involve you in a *comparison* with what you think and with other theories on writing.

typical instructions for a discussion may be:

argue	propose and support a point of view, or weigh up and compare several views on an issue and develop a thesis
analyse	examine each part of an issue or argument
interpret	explain what is meant and relate to the topic
evaluate	make a judgement on the worth, truth, usefulness etc.
criticise / critique	analyse, examine the parts, make a judgement, weighing up positive and negative features

critically evaluate   make a judgement, weighing up positive and negative features
critically analyse   examine the parts, weighing up positive and negative features
review   in the sense of making a critical analysis
assess   make a judgement, weighing up positive and negative features
discuss   weigh up and compare several views, develop a thesis

planning to write a discussion:
using a comparison grid and free-writing

In preparing to write on this issue, you may already have a personal response before you read several different viewpoints. You may entirely agree with the proposition in the task: in other words your response is 'yes' or 'in favour'; or you may wish to entirely disagree with the statement, so that your response is 'no'. In a sense you are comparing what others write with your own views, or comparing them with each other to come to your own view.

it is useful to write the introduction last: see Part 2

For a matter to be an issue, there will be a range of views about it, and it is unlikely that there are clear-cut, 'black and white' answers. Often reading widely for an assignment and thinking it through results in the feeling of confusion as you enter the 'grey' areas of argument. A comparison grid is a useful visual strategy for teasing out differing views on issues. As mentioned earlier, use the drafting process to free-write to clarify your views, as often by the time you reach the conclusion you will have thought it through and your own thesis will have emerged. Obviously, for difficult issues with many possible interpretations, this is a time-consuming process that takes more than one drafting.

Your response may then end up with a view resting on *however*, that is, saying neither 'yes' nor 'no' to the proposition. By contrasting various views on the issue, you are more likely to end up adopting a position which balances reasons and evidence in favour of a viewpoint against those to the contrary, to determine an overall position that concedes in some areas: a 'grey' position rather than a 'black and white' one. Signal words that enable you to cross between contrasting views without seeming to contradict yourself are listed below. These are very important **to guide your readers** as they work through your argument.

signals to use in your topic sentence that help
to link your material in a discussion include:

on the one hand ... ; on the other ... ; however ... ; although ... ; despite ... ; The strength of this view ... ; The advantages of this ... ; A positive contribution to the debate ... ; The disadvantages ... ; The negative effects ... ; This view ignores/emphasises/is limited by ...

tense and pronoun choice

Language choices: use the timeless present tense as the discussion is on-going, even if research you refer to is quite old! A theory still 'says' the same thing, whenever it is read. Usually a discussion is written in the third person to suggest objectivity; certainly a sense of personal distance from the topic is advisable. Of course if you have been invited by the wording of the assignment to include your own views, use first person but be sure that your arguments are well-reasoned and well-founded on research or other writers' theorising with which you agree. Responses that are not well-considered are unlikely to be valued.

A useful way to organise a discussion of an issue follows.

writing the essay

model discussion essay

Today's university students are not well-equipped for the demands of Australia in the 21st century. Discuss.

introduction: plan by sentences

tell them what you're going to tell them!

» a general statement about the issue under discussion, with reference to the task: *In the 21st century ... concerns in some parts of the Australian community that universities are failing to prepare their students for the future.*
» identify the issues being debated (in the order in which the essay is structured)
» Issue 1. ... *universities are failing to prepare their students for the future (Are they? Who says?)*
» Issue 2. ... *skills of critical analysis and discernment are even more essential ... basic necessity for personal as well as professional life in a world of rapid change (Why? Who says?)*
» Issue 3. ... *find a balance between providing sufficient vocational content in a course and teaching the skills of critical analysis ... requiring innovative approaches to integrating one with the other ...*
» Issue 4. ...*Without a focus on such skills ... Australian universities will have failed*
» define any significant terms:
  1. *exponential changes in technology and science, the so-called information explosion*
  2. *the material knowledge of their profession ... sufficient vocational content in a course*
  3. *develop critical capacities ... skills of critical analysis and discernment ...*
» preview your own point of view (thesis) and reasons for it: *Without a focus on such skills, however, graduates may find themselves unable to adapt to a world of rapid change and Australian universities will have failed.*
» you may also need to explain the scope or limits of your discussion: *In the 21st century ... Australian ... some international comparisons ...*

Here is the full introduction showing how it previews the assignment to come and uses the key words of the task:

In the 21st century, exponential changes in technology and science, and the so-called information explosion, mean that today's graduates have more to learn than ever before, raising concerns in some parts of the Australian community that universities are failing to prepare their students for the future. Although it has always been the case that students should learn not only the material knowledge of their profession but develop critical capacities as well, in the current context, skills of critical analysis and discernment are even more essential. Indeed, recent research suggests that these skills are a basic necessity for personal as well as professional life in a world of rapid change. It is difficult for universities to find a balance between providing sufficient vocational content in a course and teaching the skills of critical analysis, and some international comparisons suggest it is a common problem, requiring innovative approaches to integrate one with the other. Without a focus on such skills, however, graduates may find themselves unable to adapt to a world of rapid change and Australian universities will have failed.

model discussion essay *continued*

tell them! } ### body: plan by paragraphs

Use a comparison table or grid in planning paragraphs. Each cell in the table represents a paragraph of the body, and can be rearranged until you are satisfied there is a logical order. For a new point, take a new paragraph. A suggested paragraph structure follows. (An essay of this nature would, of course, require more than three sources; space limits this model but the strategies remain relevant.)

planning by using a comparison grid of theorists' views on which to base your view.

ISSUE	Writer A: newspaper columnist	Writer B: researcher	Writer C: researcher	Therefore I think..
1. Knowledge explosion – describe and explain	Emotive – claims unis failing – some statistics?	Examples – claims unis coping – surveys of graduates and employers	Examples of changing demands of work. Theoretical definitions.	Consensus about situation. Evidence from B & C refute A – reasons for A's views?
2. Critical skills equip students	Silent	Definitions and examples	International evidence agrees	Sum up findings – how to achieve?
3. Balance vocational with critical skills	Anecdotes – largely negative	Overseas examples. Balancing difficulties, research findings.	Overseas comparisons	A reflects concerns despite evidence
4. Implications for Australia	Gloom and doom	Role of research – examples of universities achieving balanced curriculum	Emphasis on strategies for life-long work	Sum up challenges – time constraints, resources, a balance

Par 1: first issue: Knowledge explosion.

Elaborate on the current situation – causes of the knowledge explosion. Agreement of three sources (A, B & C). Writer A suggests Australian universities failing to cope in this context. Give evidence from A (acknowledge sources with in-text referencing).

> *While there is common agreement that Australia faces new challenges (A, B, C) ...*
> *One commentator (A) maintains ... in the current climate of ...*

Par 2: opposing view on first issue: Contrary evidence.

Writer C (acknowledge sources with in-text referencing) –
> *On the other hand it is strongly suggested (C) that Australian universities are coping when it is taken into account that ... and recent surveys*

model discussion essay continued

indicating graduate satisfaction (B) and employer satisfaction (B) indicate the success of ... furthermore, the actual reasons for the claims made by A could be ...

Par 3: second issue: Critical skills essential in the light of previous point.

Considerable evidence from writers B and C; give details (acknowledge sources with in-text referencing). Writer A is silent on this issue.

In the light of the demands of the current context, there is consensus that programs concentrating on critical skills enhance learning ... (B, C). ... while C has demonstrated the long-term effect of ... In addition it has been shown overseas that ... (C) and that ... (B, C)

Par 4 & 5: third issue: How to balance teaching vocational content with critical skills?

Contrast the research evidence from Australia and overseas as cited by writers B and C with the opinions of A (acknowledge sources with in-text referencing).

However, significant comparisons with overseas universities indicate ... and reveal ... (B, C). Compared to ... it is clear that ... (C). While A's sources are largely anecdotal, nevertheless he highlights significant concerns felt in the Australian community (A) ...

Par 6 & 7: fourth issue: Possible implications in Australia; summary of main arguments from writers A, B and C (acknowledge sources with in-text referencing).

Despite differences in their views ... A, B and C agree that the next generations of graduates face ... C particularly outlines the strategies needed for life-long work ... the need for resources such as ... (C) and of a clearer understanding of the connection between learning information, and learning skills to evaluate it ... (B) the role of research ...

tell them what you've told them!

conclusion: plan by sentences

» link your thesis to the wording of the task: *... preparedness of graduates from Australian universities to meet the demands of the 21st century, it has been suggested that universities are failing.*

» sum up your argument and restate your thesis (refer to the wording of your introduction to check that you have not modified your view, and if you have, redraft your introduction to match): *... when programs focusing on critical competence are integrated into professional course work, graduates gain life-long skills.*

» draw an implication, mention the significance or your recommendations if appropriate: *skills that enable them to deal with the rapidly changing demands of their work, and perhaps of their personal life as well.*

» do not add any new evidence or examples in the conclusion.

Finally, here is an example of a conclusion showing a balancing of the parts of the essay and a final position taken by the writer (in alignment with one of the researchers):

model discussion essay continued

In the light of some Australian and overseas evidence, it is clear that when programs focusing on critical competence are integrated into professional course work, graduates gain life-long skills that enable them to deal with the rapidly changing demands of their work, and perhaps of their personal life as well. Universities then cannot be accused of failure. Issues of time constraints and achieving a satisfactory balance in the curriculum must be met and it is essential that such programs are not isolated to a few universities. In the complex debate over the preparedness of graduates from Australian universities to meet the demands of the 21st century, greater understanding of and increased resources for these programs are essential.

There is a full example of another discussion essay at the end of this book. It was brainstormed, mindmapped and drafted many times. It was only finished when the deadline arrived! You may want to read it as a model of :
» the development of an argument
» the connection between the introduction and conclusion
» topic sentences and cohesive ties between paragraphs
» in-text referencing, direct quotes
» paraphrasing
» a reference list and bibliography

checklist

→ new point in the argument means a new paragraph - see Part 2: *paragraphing*
→ start each paragraph with a topic sentence to indicate the relevance of the point and to signal the reason for the following information
→ integrate the relevant research and arguments of the writers either using the writer's name directly: e.g. *... as research evidence from Australia and overseas as cited by writers B and C* or indirectly: e.g. *Surveys indicating graduate satisfaction* (B).
→ relate the contrasting views to your own thesis using signal words to indicate your position
→ sum up a lengthy paragraph with a concluding sentence.

4.

academic writing is . . .

writing the report

purpose and audience

recognising types of reports:
  experiential
  information
  research

strategies for starting a report

sections of the report:
  introduction
  body
  » *method / methodology*
  » *findings / results / data*
  » *discussion / analysis*
  conclusion
  » *recommendations/implications*

using graphical material: figures and tables

reference list and bibliography

supplementary parts / endmatter
  glossary & list of acronyms
  adding an appendix

checklist

discourse is used here to refer to the way language is used by and among people in a specific context

In this section, individual parts of a report are explained with examples. Further information can also be found in Part 5: *making it 'sound' academic*, Part 6: *text types* and Part 7: *referencing*. This section needs to be read in conjunction with particular assignment instructions and your Faculty Referencing Guidelines or online university guides (see Part 7: *referencing*) as there may be differences due to discipline-specific discourses. Underlying all decisions of content and formatting should be two questions: What does the reader need to know? What is the clearest way to inform that reader?

purpose and audience

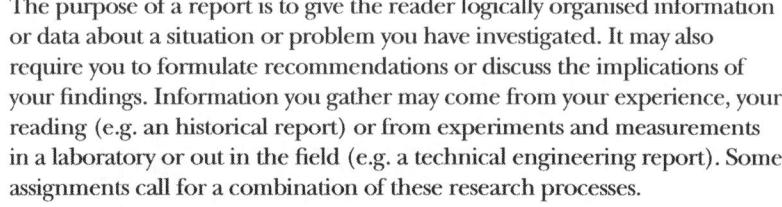

purpose and audience: see Part 1

The purpose of a report is to give the reader logically organised information or data about a situation or problem you have investigated. It may also require you to formulate recommendations or discuss the implications of your findings. Information you gather may come from your experience, your reading (e.g. an historical report) or from experiments and measurements in a laboratory or out in the field (e.g. a technical engineering report). Some assignments call for a combination of these research processes.

An initialism occurs when initials are not pronounced as a word, such as UTS. An acronym is a word made from initials, such as TAFE.

You need to be clear about the audience of your writing; for example, an assignment might specify that you imagine a non-specialist readership (such as the general public) or conversely, you may be writing for specialists in your field in a scholarly research journal. How much information and how much context you need to give, and your choice of technical or non-technical language, will depend on this audience and your purpose. You may need to provide a glossary to assist the reader with unfamiliar terms, initialisms or a list of acronyms (explained at the end of Part 4). Refer to Part 5: *technical terms* for further suggestions of appropriate language choices.

Generally, report assignments expect a predictable progression of steps in an investigation where material is clearly sectioned into specific parts, each with its own purpose and language conventions.

the arrangement of
→ **HEADING**
→ **Subheading**
→ **Sub-subheading**
is called a hierarchy

The use of a hierarchy of headings, subheadings and numbered or dot points signals this progression to guide the reader. Some computer programs are useful in sorting parts of a text into a hierarchy but this should be done last, when you are satisfied that each section and subsection makes sense in the overall schema of the report. The use of visual markers such as font changes (bold type, italics) and white space assist the reader to locate and focus on particular parts, and graphical material can be used to illustrate the findings. Beware of breaking the text up too much, however, as readers still require connections and predictability for comprehension (see Part 3: *cohesion & choosing the text type – essay or report?*).

Part 3 has explained some of the differences between academic writing for an essay and a report, in which a list of dot or numbered points makes information more accessible than a series of sentences. However, unlike sections where it is appropriate to list and number information, some sections of a report do require essay writing conventions: for example, a literature review, an analysis and discussion of your findings/experience, and your conclusions, based on your evidence. You also need to give the reader an overview of the contents (the abstract or executive summary,

which has its own conventions), possibly appendixes of additional data (see below) and a reference list and/or a bibliography. For details and examples, see:
» Part 3: *essay writing*
» Part 6: *the abstract, the executive summary, the literature review*
» Part 7: *reference list & bibliography*

recognising types of reports

an experiential report: writing about an experience

In some assignments the instruction to 'write a report' may mean that you retell a recent learning experience such as in a classroom, on a ward, or on a site. It may require a description of your day-to-day experience as well as information that you collect about the practices in that location. Your purpose is to organise that experience in a logical and clear manner for your reader, who may have set specific questions or tasks about your experience. Use these questions as headings, as a useful way to signal your responses. Your **Table of Contents** should match the sequence or structure of these questions. For example:

> Write a report about a week's experience at university. In your analysis, include your perceptions of the value of orientation and introductory activities such as the library tour; your experience of any social activities; your first lecture and tutorial experience and any other significant experience. How did the first week's experience compare to your expectations? From your experience, what would be your advice to a new student?

A suggested table of contents for this task might use the following headings, related to the parts of the task. Check if an Abstract is needed (Part 6). The functions of each section for this task have been noted briefly here:

1. **Introduction:** outline the purpose of this report. Context: where and when? Introduce yourself – what are you studying and why? Mention the scope of the report: that is, limited to a personal view of one orientation experience at one university at a particular time. Overview of report's structure.
2. **Orientation activities:** describe and evaluate.
3. **Social activities:** describe and evaluate.
4. **First learning experiences:** describe and evaluate.
5. **Other significant experiences:** describe and evaluate.
6. **Evaluation** of overall experience and comparison with expectations.
7. **Conclusion:** advice to a new student. Reiterate main findings of your experience.

Language choices: use the past tense to retell events (e.g. *The first lecture was crowded and I could not hear* ...), and the present tense to comment on them, that is, the significance of an experience to a new student (e.g. *This suggests that new students need to arrive early to a lecture to get a seat* ...).

an information report: a briefing paper

The purpose of this type of report is usually to provide information that will enable a conclusion to be drawn, or recommendations to be made.

For example, you may be reporting an historical development or trend, or providing a background context which may be the first in a series of steps in the construction of a research report.

A hypothetical task: you have been asked to gather all the information that is available to students in their first week on campus about the services offered by the university.

Steps: group and categorise the information under suitable headings, such as online information (e.g. *Student Services information, Careers Service information, Library information*), print information, signage and help desks, and so on.

Give **definitions, classifications and descriptions** to make it easy for the reader to follow, clearly signalled by headings and numbered sections. Use graphs to make comparisons in the amount of material available under certain categories (see below).

It would be likely that you would have a section called **Analysis** where you would make comparisons. In the **Conclusion** section, sum up your findings, perhaps with **Recommendations** (such as: *More online and print information, such as leaflets, is needed to inform students regarding scholarships and bursaries*). You can see that this type of report is limited to gathering and reporting information, and so usually would form the basis of an investigation (and would perhaps justify that investigation).

Check if an Abstract is needed (Part 6).

Language choices: use the past tense for events that are over (e.g. *In previous years, students were provided with a faculty handbook ...*) and present tense to outline and analyse current information. Use the third person for impersonal reporting (e.g. *Online information is regularly updated*, not *I found it helpful that online information is regularly updated*).

research reports

The purpose of your research will determine the main areas on which you should focus and general guidelines only are given here. Check with your Faculty Referencing Guidelines, or in professional journals for models, as the focus, format and language of your report should reflect the requirements of your field (its discourse). An Abstract will be needed (see: *the abstract and executive summary*, Part 6).

In many faculties, report writing for an assignment is modelled on the sort of reports that are written in that particular profession, for example, a marketing report for a business or a technical report for an engineering company. One purpose in setting you the task of report writing may be so that you become accustomed to writing 'like an historian', or 'like an engineer' (this may suggest that all historians or all engineers write in the same way, but of course you should expect variations within any one discipline). This is seen as practice for your career, where research reports may be the basis for decisions made in that context.

A report may also be set as an assessment task in a research methodologies subject, to demonstrate your grasp of the research process and as preparation for possible later scholarly writing in honours and postgraduate courses.

writing the report 53

strategies for starting a report:

see Part 2: brainstorming, mindmapping

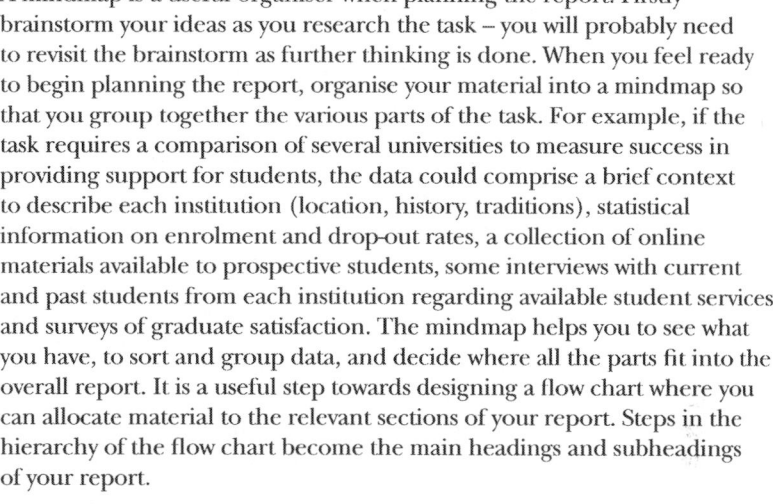

from brainstorm to mindmap to flow chart ...

order from chaos! writing is messy!

A mindmap is a useful organiser when planning the report. Firstly brainstorm your ideas as you research the task – you will probably need to revisit the brainstorm as further thinking is done. When you feel ready to begin planning the report, organise your material into a mindmap so that you group together the various parts of the task. For example, if the task requires a comparison of several universities to measure success in providing support for students, the data could comprise a brief context to describe each institution (location, history, traditions), statistical information on enrolment and drop-out rates, a collection of online materials available to prospective students, some interviews with current and past students from each institution regarding available student services, and surveys of graduate satisfaction. The mindmap helps you to see what you have, to sort and group data, and decide where all the parts fit into the overall report. It is a useful step towards designing a flow chart where you can allocate material to the relevant sections of your report. Steps in the hierarchy of the flow chart become the main headings and subheadings of your report.

This outline is mirrored on the contents page, enabling the reader to see at a glance how your material is organised. It is helpful to think of the contents page as the plan or skeleton of the report, and as a guide for sequencing the Abstract (Part 6).

sections of the report

overview of the structure of a report:

flow chart – generic sections of a report

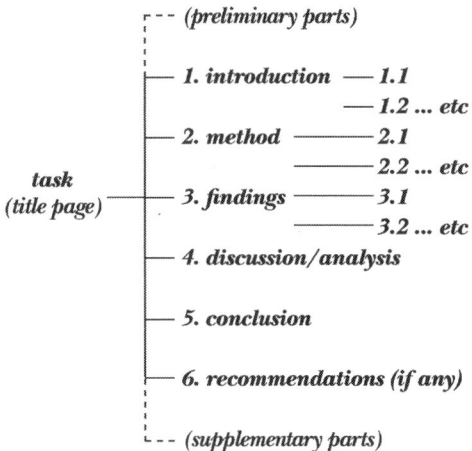

note: each subsection can be further sectioned e.g. 2.2.1; 2.2.3 ... etc. if needed

In brief, a report needs to begin with an explanation of your purpose and the context and scope of your investigation (**Introduction**). You may need to refer to other sources to provide context and a rationale (**Literature Review:** see Part 6). You then need to detail what you did in your investigation, such as interviews or experiments and any measurements or calculations (**Method**) as evidence of your work, so that, if necessary, your steps can be replicated to check for accuracy and reliability. You then need to describe what you have found (**Findings**). In technical reports your calculations may be the bulk of the report (e.g. *a comparison of chemical reactions under a range of conditions*) while in a non-technical report a survey may only play a minor role (e.g. *more students interviewed expressed a preference for assignments rather than exams*).

It is then necessary to analyse and discuss your findings (**Discussion**), and come to some conclusions (**Conclusion**), sometimes in the light of other research in the same or similar area. If relevant, you may be asked to produce some recommendations about the problem or situation you have investigated (**Recommendations**) and to discuss any implications for the future.

In addition a report will have some of the following:

Preliminary parts: Title page, Acknowledgements, Contents and Abstract. Not all tasks require an acknowledgement of those who have assisted you; be guided by models in your field and the assignment's instructions. Acknowledgements, which should be brief, are usually found on a separate page following the title page. This may be the only place where your personal voice is expected in a report (first person pronouns: see Part 5) although in some fields this is changing (see below).

Supplementary parts: Reference List and/or Bibliography (see Part 7), Appendix and Glossary. The sequence of ordering these parts varies depending on the professional field; some prefer a glossary as a preliminary part rather than at the end, and some expect the references to follow the appendixes. Conventions for including an appendix and a glossary can be found at the end of this chapter. Consult your Faculty Referencing Guidelines or ask.

Headings, subheadings and topic sentences: Each section of a report thus reflects these steps, organised into sections by the use of headings, subheadings and numbers.

Decisions on sectioning will depend on the amount of material you have and its relevance to the design of your research. A short section may be better within a larger one; a lengthy section may be easier to read if divided into logical parts and so numbered. Avoid overly fragmenting your text with too many subsets; consider the reader. Be very systematic in the formatting and numbering of sections. The hierarchy of headings and subheadings may be shown using bold, capitalised or italic text; check the preferences of your field and do not overload the text with too many variations in formatting. An alphabetical or decimal numbering system may be preferred in your field (e.g. *1.c* or *1.3*). The table of contents should exactly match the in-text formatting so check this carefully when proofreading.

topic sentence: see Part 2

Headings and subheadings in a report do the same job as topic sentences in paragraphs in essays, that is, they are signals to the reader. In addition, topic sentences are needed in reports as the first sentence in a section to connect the heading with what follows and to lead into the information. For example, if a heading is *1.1 Historical context over the past 10 years*, the following topic sentence could be: *This issue has dominated public discussion over the past ten years, when the Bloggs Report (1999) first highlighted ...*

Each field of study may have preferred variations to the above generic model (which may also vary within a faculty from subject to subject) so you should consult your Faculty Referencing Guidelines, ask your tutor for specific requirements or check online resources. This text relies on the *Style manual for authors, editors and printers* (2002), an Australian guide available in libraries and covered in more detail in Part 7: *referencing*. It is a useful resource, particularly when you move to writing lengthy reports or theses in the later years of your studies.

writing the report

an Abstract is not the same as an Introduction (Part 6)

introduction: plan by sentences

"tell them what you're going to tell them"

The purpose of the introductory paragraph/s of a report is like that of the essay, in that the first sentences establish the general issue. Each subsequent sentence narrows that issue down towards the specific objectives of the research or project, providing a predictable structure for the report.

» an overview of what is to come. For example: *It is increasingly important to identify the factors that may prevent the drop-out of university students ...*
» a rationale or justification for it. For example: *because ...*
» an outline of the context of the problem or situation you are examining. For example: <u>*This study examines*</u> *the importance of university orientation and introductory activities in building positive attitudes towards study ... in Australia at the present time ...*
» an indication of the scope or limitations of your investigation, if relevant. For example: *This research <u>is limited to</u> students attending the city campuses of three inner city universities in Sydney ...*
» a description of your aim and explicit objectives. For example:
  Aim: ... building positive attitudes towards study ... in Australia at the present time ...
  Objectives:
  1. to examine the importance of university orientation ...
  2. to examine introductory activities ...

aims and objectives } In some circumstances you may hear the terms aims and objectives used interchangeably but generally it is accepted that the aim is the broad purpose of the investigation. Objectives are some specific tasks to achieve that aim and need to be manageable tasks with achievable outcomes. In your research, try to limit them to what is possible and reasonable in the context of the assignment's parameters. An aim is a larger, longer-term ambition that could not be achieved in one small research study. However, numerous such studies can build up answers to an issue, and this is why a review of what has already been found is necessary. Part of your task may be to integrate your findings with literature in the field.

Within the introduction section you may therefore need to provide an orientation for the reader: a brief historical background or a short time-line of significant events leading up to the present investigation. It is easier for the reader if these are subsections, with subheadings such as

  1.1 Historical context: the past ten years
  1.2 Political and economic context

However, if the explanation of the context of the problem is lengthy, you may need to make entirely separate sections, such as **Background/ Context/Key Terms/Definitions**.

If you have been asked to provide an analysis of existing research, policies or theorising on the issue, you will need a subsection entitled **Literature Review**. A separate section for this purpose is probably not warranted in a short report. Reference to a few sources can instead be incorporated into the introductory paragraphs. The choices about sectioning will depend on the assignment instructions: make decisions based on giving the reader a clear understanding of what is important. If the literature review is a major part of the report, make it a separate section and see Part 6: *writing a literature review*.

Language choices: use the present tense to outline the problem, which is probably ongoing. Use the past tense to describe events that have occurred when giving a background or context. It is usual to express the aims of the project in the third person, as in *The purpose of* ... rather than *My purpose was* ...

body of the report: plan by sections

"tell them"

The usual sections found in the body of a report are explained below. Note that language conventions depend on the purpose and audience for each section. Reports written in the workplace may have a diverse readership, with some readers more interested in a particular section than another. View each section as an independent entity that makes sense as a stand-alone text. This will mean that you explain each step of your investigation thoroughly, and may also involve some repetition in the opening sentences as you remind the reader of the purpose of the study. Examples follow.

method / methodology

To tie the method to the task, an opening sentence to that section could be: *In order to establish student satisfaction with support services provided by three inner-city universities, the following sampling techniques were used ... Various qualitative methods were also used: document review, interview and questionnaire ...*

Following this brief introduction to the section, focus on details: list in order the steps or procedures undertaken in your investigation. Another researcher should be able to replicate and perhaps critique these steps.

Use subheadings to separate distinct parts, for example:
    2.1 Target group (or sample)
    2.2 Questionnaires

In simple terms, describe the process clearly and if writing a technical report, you may need to include descriptions of resources (materials, equipment etc.).

Language choices: use the past tense as the events of the method are over, and sequencing signals such as *firstly* ... ; *the second step* ... ; *finally*. It is usual to use third person pronouns and impersonal sentence structures such as passive constructions; for example, *Two hundred questionnaires were distributed* ... instead of *We distributed 200 questionnaires* ...

findings/results/data

Again, your aim should be clarity and the logical sequencing of information for your reader. Provide a linking (topic) sentence referring to the research task establishing a context for this section, such as: *The results reported in this study of student satisfaction with support services at three inner-city universities indicate similar responses to several items in the questionnaires (see table 2)* ...

However, a full discussion of the significance of your findings should be located in the Discussion section. The Findings section gives the actual results of your research, utilising graphics such as charts, tables, graphs, illustrations and photographs which may be the clearest means of demonstrating these results (see below: *using graphical material: figures and tables*). Make sure that you refer to each graphic with a brief explanation in the text and check that each is labelled and numbered consecutively.

A *List of Figures* and a *List of Tables* should also be given in your table of contents. If you have a large volume of empirical results, include them in an appendix so that the overall flow of your report is not interrupted (see *adding an appendix* below). Indicate this to the reader at the relevant point in the text, for example, *... see Appendix A*.

Language choices: use the past tense and the passive construction to describe what was found, in keeping with the impersonal tone of the report, for example: *It was found that 80% of students surveyed were ...* Use third person pronouns: *It was found ...* not *We found ...*

Comparative terms are very useful, for example: <u>More</u> *students reported positive experiences in their first week ...* and comparison tables make it manageable to show a number of comparisons across several variables at a glance. Aim to keep the prose explanations concise and logically connected.

see Part 5: making it 'sound' academic

discussion/analysis

This section of your report resembles a short essay in that it is a connected series of sentences that explain and argue for an interpretation of the evidence in the report. You may also find it strengthens your argument to refer to some of the literature that was surveyed earlier. For example:
> *From this study it is clear that students' positive attitudes towards their university studies develop in the first week of their university experience. Although the students surveyed here were representative of only three large city campuses, these findings are consistent with earlier studies carried out in regional universities (Bloggs 2007; Smith & Jones 2008) ... More research is needed ...*

Language choices: use the present tense to discuss the ongoing situation as revealed in the investigation. Some writers personalise this section to include themselves, as in: *We were surprised to discover that ...* There is a trend to personalise in this way in some disciplines and the decision to write personally depends largely on the tradition and practices in that discipline, which you should check with your lecturer and in current professional reports and journals.

no new material should be introduced into the conclusion

conclusion: plan by sentences

"tell them what you've told them"

This section resembles the conclusion of an essay as its purpose is a summary to remind the reader of:
» the overall purpose of the report (check with your introduction, aim/s and objectives)
» the steps through which it has progressed (check your method section)
» its overall findings and point of view. Here you may make generalisations based on your evidence, which leads to
» the recommendations (if numerous, make a separate section: see below).
For example:
> *This study has investigated ... in the context of ... and it has found ... On the basis of this evidence ...*

recommendations/implications

If the purpose of the report has been to identify actions to be taken as a result of the findings, these should be listed here. It is usual that recommendations are numbered in a logical sequence, for example:

It is therefore recommended that:
1. *Orientation activities should be advertised by ...*
2. *First year students should be surveyed in second semester for their views on ...*

and so on. In some business reports, the list of recommendations may follow the executive summary at the beginning of the report, on the assumption that the reader wants to know this information from the start. If there is only a general recommendation such as 'further research is needed', it should be incorporated into the conclusion and/or discussion sections.

Language choices: use the past tense to review what the report found, and move into the present tense to comment. Terms such as *should* or *must* suggest actions to be taken. It is usual to keep to the third person as in the previous example, although in some fields there is a tendency to personalise recommendations, such as:

On the basis of this research, we believe that:
1. *Orientation activities should be advertised by ...*
2. *First year students should be surveyed in second semester for ...*

using graphical material: figures and tables

Figures: Another significant feature of a report may be its use of graphical material such as charts, graphs or diagrams called figures, though this may depend on the conventions of the discipline. Photographs, maps and illustrations may sometimes be included as figures. See also the *Style manual for authors, editors and printers* (2002) mentioned in Part 7 as a useful guide for and detailed explanation of a variety of figures and illustrations. As previously mentioned, there are discipline-specific conventions in report writing, so check Faculty Referencing Guidelines or ask.

If you rely on a very large number of figures or tables as evidence for assertions (for example, a large volume of statistical material, experimental findings or observational notes) it may be more appropriate to group them together, clearly numbered and labelled as an appendix. In this way the written text will not be excessively interrupted, and a signal such as *see Appendix* at the appropriate place in the text will direct the reader to consult the relevant data. Readers may not always study the detail within the appendixes, but they must be there as evidence of the data relied on in the report.

a reader-friendly text? }   The decision to use a graph or diagram should be based on the ease of reading that it provides compared to a wordy explanation, particularly if it sums up a trend, a change or a comparison. Each figure should be given a label or title and numbered, such as: *Figure 4. Line graph indicating student satisfaction over a 6 month period.* This could be written above or below the figure, depending on faculty preferences. Be sure to locate the figure as closely as possible to the relevant text, with a cross-reference such as:

... as can be seen in Figure 4, student satisfaction increased ...
or: *Student satisfaction increased ... (see Figure 4) ...*

Some faculties expect you to include a *List of Figures* in the table of contents if they are numerous. Proofread carefully so that numbers, titles and choices of bold or italics match the body of your text exactly.

writing the report

too much? }

Unfortunately, the availability of sophisticated computer-generated graphics often encourages a tendency to put every finding into a pie-chart, line graph, or bar chart. Although this may initially look impressive, the discerning reader will soon realise that there is not enough data to warrant an elaborate graphic; the message would be simpler in text. Alternatively, too much data contained in a single figure can be like a roadblock to meaning. Like the paragraph test, relevance to audience and purpose must be the deciding factor. If graphics confuse, distract or overwhelm the reader, communication has broken down.

Tables: The conventions for using comparison tables in a report are similar to those for figures. Some disciplines do not differentiate between the two categories, while others require a separate *List of Tables* in the contents page. Proofread carefully so that numbers, titles and choices of bold or italics match the body of your text exactly.

See also the *Style manual* mentioned in Part 7 as a useful guide for and detailed explanations of a variety of tables, and for discipline-specific conventions in report writing, check Faculty Referencing Guidelines or ask. Restraint is important in choosing tabular form for information: avoid too little or too much. Your audience and purpose must be your guide to what is necessary.

Within the text, all comparison tables should be labelled and numbered such as:

Table 3. Comparison of positive responses to item 1 of the questionnaire, by Faculty.

and positioned as closely as possible to the relevant part of the written text. Make reference to the table so that the reader understands why it is there and what it signifies. Wording such as *See Table 3*, or *as shown in Table 3* will guide the reader to the relevant graphic.

reference list and bibliography

see Part 7 }

The references used in the report need to alphabetically listed here, and if instructed, a bibliography of extra sources may follow.

supplementary parts / endmatter

glossary & list of acronyms

Conventions vary as to the order of endmatter such as this, but it is recommended that they come after the body of the report rather than before, as a reference source the reader may or may not need. It is usual to include a glossary where there are many terms in the report requiring definition but not if there is a limited number, when it is better to define these within the context of the text, or in a brief subsection in the introduction.

plural of appendix is appendixes or appendices

adding an appendix

An appendix is a way to include extra material for the reader to consider at the end of your report, such as material that you judge will interrupt the flow of information. It may be information that is not essential in the body of the report itself, but is relevant, for example, because it adds to the context. However in some cases it may be evidential material on which your findings are based, such as statistical calculations or data from another source (e.g. the Australian Bureau of Statistics) and these must be provided for the reader to verify.

An appendix may be a copy of a document, such as a letter of permission to conduct an interview, or a blank copy of a survey form used in the investigation. Be aware of issues of privacy and confidentiality that may be raised in including some documents in your appendixes and check these requirements with your tutor. It may be appropriate to label such a document with a person's title rather than by name, such as *Appendix 2: Notes from an interview with a Student Association member*. It is essential that in the relevant part of the body of the report, you specify what material can be found in an appendix, for example, ... *see Appendix 2* or *as shown in Appendix D* ...

Each appendix should begin on a separate page and be listed in the table of contents by title and number, though some faculties prefer appendices to be alphabeticised. This section usually follows the report's reference list (and bibliography, if there is one).

checklist

→ table of contents matches the hierarchy of formatting of the report: font style (eg. bold/capitals/italics), indentations etc. and page numbers are provided
→ abstract or executive summary is clearly structured by sentences to match the sequences of the report
→ introduction sets a clear purpose, context and the scope of the report
→ aims and objectives as stated in the introduction are referred to in the findings and discussion in the same sequence
→ all sources are accurately acknowledged in the text and reference list
→ sections of the report are clearly labelled and follow language conventions (tense, active or passive constructions etc.)
→ figures and tables are referred to in the text, labelled and located appropriately, and are listed in the table of contents
→ discussion section ties together the findings and the issues and leads to the conclusion and recommendations (if any)
→ conclusion reiterates the introduction and leads to the recommendations (if any)
→ appendixes are separately collated and referred to appropriately in the text.

5.

academic writing is . . .
making it 'sound' academic

levels of academic writing
writing from a personal perspective
writing from an academic distance
  what comes first in a sentence
  verb choice
  pronoun choice
  active or passive construction
  abstract nouns
  technical terms
  nominalisation
  tentative tone
getting the balance
combining personal and distanced writing
objectivity?

Imagine the most personal writing that you might do – a secret diary, a reminder list with abbreviations, idioms, symbols – not intended for another reader – writing as you think or speak, in fragments and disconnected chunks – a 'stream of consciousness' style – highly personal. Like this text!

Imagine at the other extreme a legal document, which is a written text, worked on and perhaps argued over for some time as individuals or groups endeavour to remove any ambiguities to ensure that it stands independently for all time, outlining rights and responsibilities, terms and conditions, in complex, technical and highly structured language which may be difficult for an outsider to understand, as exemplified here.

be in a position to choose your style

Inexperienced writers are frequently told to improve their style. Preoccupation with content, the **what** of the writing, may leave little energy or time to think about style, the **how** of it. Often students are concerned that their conversational tone does not 'sound' academic – as one student expressed the dilemma: "It is easier to write like you speak than write like you read!" At the other end of the spectrum, students from formal educational or vocational backgrounds may be uncomfortable with any level of informality in their writing. It is essential that students have a repertoire of styles from which to choose for the demands of different tasks. The strategies described below are intended to present these choices so that writers are not restricted to one way of writing which may not be appropriate for a task.

levels of academic writing

clarity, clarity, clarity!

The range of assignments you may be asked to write should be seen as different texts for different purposes. Imagine a continuum, or sliding scale which 'measures the level' of formality of any text. At one end would be the most informal or personal style of writing, at the other end the most formal writing you can think of (see the examples at the beginning of this section – which are not recommended for you to copy! You may know of more extreme examples than these). Academic writing would be located between the two extremes; some assignments are more personalised, others more formal in tone and style. You should avoid the two extremes as clear communication is essential in your assignments.

The choice that proficient writers make about the level of formality of a text depends on their purpose in writing and their intended audience for the text; for example, consider how successful advertisers and politicians pitch their texts to a particular level. When writing for academic purposes, the style of the writing is determined by an interpretation of the task, and by what seems to be expected by the lecturer or tutor assessing your assignment. With an awareness of particular words (vocabulary) and grammar (sentence structure) you can achieve either an informal or a more formal tone in your text. Some of the language features that help to create an informal or a formal tone and style are listed below. This table is not intended to represent academic writing as an 'either ... or' choice, as if there are only two ways to write; often one assignment requires you to switch back and forth between the levels. Instead, the aim here is to show that a message (for example, your essay or report) can be changed from

making it 'sound' academic: tone and style 63

one level of formality to another by changes in its language features, with you in control, and without sacrificing clarity.

The table below gives a general indication of the style of language expected in a variety of academic text types. The terms in the table are explained throughout this section with examples.

features of informal academic language	features of formal academic writing
information based on experience:	information based on research:
focus on **the self**, using pronouns: *I, we, you*	focus on what others say/write, using pronouns: *it, they, them*
familiar vocabulary, concrete terms	technical/specialised vocabulary, abstracts
active constructions: specific events e.g. *In the first session we decided ...*	passive constructions: generalisations about abstract concepts e.g. *Decisions were made ...*
events are stated: e.g. *Students met and discussed the first topic.*	ideas may be tentatively put forward e.g. *On the basis of research it may be seen that ...*

↓ ↓

text types of informal academic writing	text types of formal academic writing
reflective journals	essays/reports that inform
autobiographies	essays/reports that argue and evaluate
experiential reports	research reports
narratives & anecdotes in case studies	explanations & analyses in case studies

for details on each text type, see Part 6

Most university assignments are located towards the more formal end of the continuum, although for personal journals and reflections you would select the more informal text features. See below *writing from a personal perspective* and see also Part 6: *the reflective journal*.

drafting see Part 2: understanding your writing process

Often you may find it useful to write informally in a stream-of-consciousness process to get started on your first draft, that is, a free-write. You may wish to make the final draft more impersonal and you can try the suggestions below, in *writing from an academic distance*. This does not mean an assignment should read like a legal document, but that it has moved beyond the personal tone of, say, a letter, towards a well-structured, clearly expressed and reasonable discussion or explanation that can be read without difficulty at any time in the future.

This book moves along the continuum between informal commentary and more formal examples of writing for academic assignments. Different audience, different purpose!

You may have noticed that this book is not very formal in style; it is not a scholarly presentation of information, acknowledging its sources at every step. However its assertions about the writing process, genres and strategies are well-supported by research listed in the bibliography, another feature of academic writing. This text uses 'you' frequently to directly address the reader, defined as the beginning writer in a university context (the intended audience) in giving explanations and asking questions. Sometimes it uses exclamations for humour or emphasis, and an occasional sentence fragment for brevity. These choices are appropriate to its purpose, that is, to give accessible advice. Therefore the writing features of the commentaries in this text are not the features recommended for your academic writing! **The examples are.**

writing from a personal perspective

1st person pronoun
I   me   my   mine
we   us   our/s

2nd person pronoun
you   your/s

3rd person pronoun
he   him   his
she   her/s
it   its
they   them   their/s

When writers want the reader to be involved and to identify with their message, they will frequently use such language devices as the second person pronoun 'you', questions and exclamations and emotive vocabulary. Read advertising material or political electioneering: such writing abounds with rhetorical devices to provoke responses and identification. For example:

1. *You ought to be congratulated!* (an advertising slogan) Grammatical features: 2nd person pronoun, an exclamation.
2. *Have you thought where a vote for the X party will leave this country? In serious debt, plagued by division!* (any political slogan) Grammatical features: 2nd person pronoun, a question, an exclamation, an incomplete sentence, emotive vocabulary.

Personal pronouns outlined in the margin note are important tools for creating a personal or impersonal tone. Some make writing 'sound' like conversation between writer and reader. For example, you may be invited to enter a dialogue with your tutor (e.g. a digital interactive task) and so it would be appropriate to use the second person pronoun 'you'. Check the task you have been set and proofread carefully for consistency. For further detail, see Part 8.

In the following descriptions of a variety of personal writing assignments, consider your reader so that you communicate clearly. You should avoid:

» a colloquial tone, slang or terms which are unfamiliar to the reader. This may confuse or annoy.
» disconnected fragments, leaving out the connections between ideas. This may make the writing incomprehensible.

It is also easy in this sort of writing to assume the reader understands and therefore to leave out parts of explanations. Although you may be requested to write in a personal tone, if a lecturer or tutor will be assessing your writing, it has to have a structure that can be followed.

In an assignment such as an autobiography or reflective essay, personal writing and an informal tone may be appropriate to express your feelings, but the task probably expects you to analyse them as well. You could read autobiographies from your discipline area to get a sense of how it is done, or ask questions. In most cases, even a personal task like this is expected to have some of the features of more formal writing, because you have an audience; the resulting text may be a mix of personal and more impersonal writing (see: *the case study*).

Note that a journal may refer to personal writing like a diary, or to the professional and scholarly journals of specific disciplines found online or in the library. See Part 6: the reflective journal

see: establishing a clear structure

A reflective journal itself may be set as an assignment for assessment. It is of course appropriate to use the 'I' pronoun in describing personal experiences or feelings in a subjective manner: you are then a direct participant in the text. Another task may require a journal/diary that itself is not for assessment, but is to be the basis for a subsequent essay or report; it would probably contain notes of your observations, feelings, and what you may have learnt. For example: *Keep a journal and record your experiences and feelings about your first week's experience in the university.* The journal thus provides the data for later writing. However the essay or report based on this material should move further along the continuum towards more formal language conventions. This becomes a different text to the original journal although you may be quoting from it, just as you may be citing other authors to support a claim or a finding. Treat the journal notes as a primary source with a separate identity to the essay or report.

If most of your writing experience has been located at the personal end of the continuum, you may quite consciously need to examine the features of more formal language and to try out some of the suggestions in this section – unless of course you have been asked to write an advertising or political slogan! The aim is not to bureaucratise your writing, but to move it gently towards an academically appropriate style.

writing from an academic distance

clarity is the first priority

To write 'academically' in this sense requires you to examine your sentence structures and vocabulary to try to achieve the desired tone. This is probably best done in a nearly-final draft when you are checking through an assignment in readiness for the intelligent stranger. If you become concerned with individual sentence construction too early in the drafting stage you may be distracted from clarifying your meaning, which must be the first priority. It is better to write simple sentences than long and convoluted ones, so if you find the following suggestions confusing, stay with simpler constructions.

On the other hand, if you wish to have your assignment 'sound academic' (and if this is what is valued in your discipline and expected in your assignment), some suggestions follow with examples. Grammatical explanations have been kept to a minimum.

'Sounding academic' is often achieved by combining some or all of the following elements, which are explained in detail below:
» the initial focus of a sentence is on the issue, not the writer
» pronoun choice positions the reader at a distance
» verb choice is precise
» the passive construction is sometimes used
» abstract nouns are more common
» technical terms are expected where relevant
» nominalisation may be used where the text focuses on ideas or concepts (things) rather than happenings (verbs)
» a tentative tone may be used.

what comes first in the sentence?

It is useful to understand that in English, what comes first in the sentence (called the Theme in some grammar books) takes the focus: it is the subject. If *I* comes first then obviously the writer is placing him/herself as the starting point, as in *I think* ... On the other hand, if the issue, or a theorist's name comes first, then this is the subject of the writing. For example, compare the three following sentences. What is the essay-writer's **initial focus** in each sentence?

1. *I think that Bloggs's (1997) explanation of the writing process provides a useful basis for understanding how to plan an assignment.*

The essay-writer is the subject, and the actual opinion is new information.

*see Part 7:
in-text citation*

2. *Bloggs's (1997) explanation of the process provides a useful basis for understanding how to plan an assignment.*

Here Bloggs takes the focus. The writer of the essay has disappeared although the opinion is still there, expressed in 'useful'.

3. *Understanding how to plan an assignment emerges from research on the writing process (Bloggs, 1997).*

Now the issue takes the focus and Bloggs, the theorist, is given less prominence. Again, the writer of the essay has disappeared and the statement sounds more authoritative than the original version.

You need to decide where you want the focus to be. It is useful to read someone else's writing (for example, a journal article or a political speech in a newspaper) to analyse where the writer has placed the focus. For example, in the two sentences that follow, what has the writer chosen to write first in the sentence, and why?

*Interviewer:
Are you going to raise taxes, Prime Minister?
PM: A decision about taxes has been made in consideration of many factors ...*

1. *I have decided that taxes should be reduced.* (The writer features him/herself first, possibly to take the credit for a popular decision.)
2. *Taxes will be increased.* (The focus is on taxes and the person who has made the decision has disappeared from the sentence, obviously not wanting to take responsibility quite so clearly! (See *active or passive construction* below).

The decision to be accountable for an action, or not, can be seen in the choice of what comes first in many sentences you will hear or read.

In academic writing, by mentioning the issue or topic in the focus position the writer creates a more formal and distant tone, which also may give more authority to the statement.

pronoun choice

See *writing from a personal perspective*, above.

Although it is improbable that anyone could write something in an entirely neutral manner, nevertheless you will often be expected to be **objective** in your writing. The reader may not expect you to be a participant in the text and your own views and personal reactions may not be explicitly wanted as in an *I believe* ... sort of statement. Avoid the first person pronouns (*I, we*).

*write about:
3rd person*

*write to:
2nd person*

*write as:
1st person*

It is expected that you have researched the topic and have evaluated various viewpoints to argue for a particular view, or to explain a process or theory. When the focus is on an issue, or the theories of researchers in an area, more impersonal wording such as *It has been suggested that* ... suggests a **more authoritative** analysis. Use the third person pronoun (*it, they*) to achieve distance.

If the focus is on information or issues, the reader probably does not expect to be included in the text either. For example, *you will agree* ... will they? *you should* ... should they? Avoid the second person pronoun (*you*). Most university writing is expected to use the third person pronoun, where you write **about** something or someone, rather than write **to** them (as in a letter). In this way, you are positioned from a distance without personal involvement in the subject.

In academic writing, unless specifically invited to participate in the text, keep to the third person pronouns and proofread carefully for consistency.

verb choice

Ensure that the verbs you choose convey a precise meaning. Some verb groups tend to be colloquial and imprecise, such as *The writer looks at the issue*. A more formal choice would be: *The writer examines (or considers) the issue*. Other examples follow:

> Informal choices: *He says ... talks about ... Evidence shows ... and you will see ...*
> Formal choices: *He states ... discusses ... maintains ... contends ... Evidence indicates ... demonstrates ... it can be explained ...*

see Part 8: verb tense

In academic writing, verbs are usually in the timeless or universal present tense indicating that the academic debate is on-going, not over. Often the interest is not so much in what people do/did, but in what it means/signifies and how it can be explained.

active or passive construction

Linked to a choice about what to put first in the sentence is the decision whether to use an active or passive sentence construction. Put simply, an active construction means that the 'doer' or agent of the action is the subject of the sentence, as in sentence 1 above: *I have decided that taxes should be reduced.*

Consider another example: *I drove over the cat. I* takes the focus and it is clear *I* did the deed, *I* am the agent. If in this scenario the deed was accidental, it is unlikely that the agent would phrase the information this way and so have to take the blame for it; more likely it would be passively constructed as in *The cat has been killed*. Now the focus is on the cat, although the cat is certainly not the agent of the deed. In fact, by focusing on the cat, the reader or listener's attention is drawn to the cat, and it may even be blamed for the accident! We may suspect that politicians and bureaucrats use the passive construction to avoid disclosing the agent of an unpopular action, but in everyday interactions, people frequently use the passive construction to stay on good terms with each other – avoiding confrontation, appearing to be rude or being held accountable. The passive can soften a difficult message.

Using the passive to be polite!
"Your writing could be improved."
→ *translation: Your writing is awful!*
"Those dirty coffee cups should be washed."
→ *translation: Wash your dirty coffee cups!*
"Emphasis has been placed on punctuality."
→ *translation: Be on time!*

In academic writing the choice of a passive construction may be made for several reasons:
» the agent is not known, or it is not necessary or important in the context to identify the agent. For example: *Essay writing can be divided into expository and argumentative texts*. (By whom? Is it relevant to know?)
» the focus is on issues not particular individuals. For example: *Care must be taken to avoid plagiarism*. (Is it necessary to say by whom? Can it be taken for granted?)
» the writer does not want to create a personal tone and so uses the passive to make a point without using the first person pronoun *I*. For example: *Writing academically is seen as a complex process ...* (in other words, *I see academic writing as a complex process...*)

abstract nouns

An abstract noun is the label in grammar for words expressing ideas, concepts and feelings, as opposed to labels for concrete and tangible things. Commonly, academic analysis is concerned with the broader, more general issues that arise from particular concrete experiences. In a case study, for example, a writer may begin with a focus on the specific event or happening (e.g. *a group of students writing an assignment*) in order to widen the discussion to issues that may arise (e.g. *the nature of the learning that is taking place or the effect of anxiety on writing performance*). Abstract nouns make this transition clear (*the nature, the learning, the effect, the anxiety, the performance*).

Your writing will 'sound' more formal and academic, as the following comparison shows, where sentence 1 focuses on people and events (concrete nouns and verbs) much in the way that you might speak, while sentence 2 translates the message into a more formal tone, like an official memo (abstract nouns are underlined in sentence 2):

1. Lecturers are talking about how many students are plagiarising from the Internet. Lecturers will have to make the rules tougher and make more frequent electronic checks. (This is a text about what people are doing and will do.)
2. Lecturers' <u>concern</u> about the <u>extent</u> of <u>student plagiarism</u> from the Internet will result in a <u>strengthening</u> of rules and increased <u>frequency</u> of electronic checking.

Try placing *the* in front of each of the underlined words and you will see the abstract nouns that make it a text about concepts and issues: *the concern, the extent, the plagiarism, the strengthening, the frequency, the checking*. As stated earlier, however, this formalising process should not be overdone.

In academic writing, the use of abstract nouns enables you to analyse, explain and evaluate concepts and theories, moving from a specific instance to a general discussion. See Part 6.

technical terms

Using technical terms in academic writing depends on the purpose and audience of the text. If writing a professional report, technical language demonstrates your expertise and will often save lengthy explanations. A glossary at the end of a report is useful for the reader when there are numerous technical terms, initialisms and acronyms to be explained.

You have to decide when definitions are needed in the light of your reader. Provide definitions early in your text unless you can take it for granted that your reader is familiar with a particular term. A problem of communication may also arise when a word has both a common meaning and a more specialised one in a particular field (e.g. culture). Be sure your meaning is clear with a definition or through the context. This will make your assumptions available to the reader, who can follow your explanation or argument even if not agreeing with your definition, making dialogue possible.

Sometimes writers are accused of using jargon, which has come to signify an excessive use of technical language. This charge usually means that the audience of the text feels excluded, even annoyed by the writer's language choices; in other words, the writer has not understood his/her audience.

In academic writing, use technical terminology when it is essential for your purpose and check the assumptions you may be making about your

Macquarie Dictionary's definition of jargon shows how the word has both a neutral meaning (language of a particular profession) and a derogatory meaning (unintelligible; gibberish).

*An **initialism** occurs when initials are not pronounced as a word, such as UTS. An **acronym** is a word made from initials, such as TAFE.*

audience. Clarity is essential in complex technical writing so pay particular attention to predictable structuring of information (see Parts 3 & 4).

nominalisation

This refers to the process of writing more abstractly, that is, by transforming concrete terms (verbs which tell about what is done and by implication, the people who have done the deeds) into language about ideas and concepts (that is, into abstract nouns). This process enables you to focus on concepts rather than events. For example:

1. *When you compare the two essays you will see that the earlier text was written in a more conversational style.*

Here it is clear who is doing what (*you are comparing*). The writing is quite direct and familiar, addressing the reader. It has the features of a spoken message.

To make it more distant in tone, and therefore more formal, the verb can be nominalised, that is made into the noun form (*compare > comparison*).

2. *A comparison of the two essays indicates that the earlier text was written in a more conversational style.*

The emphasis is thus on the abstract idea of a comparison because it comes first in the sentence, rather than on who is doing what. The pronoun (you) has disappeared and the imprecise verb (will see) has been replaced. See above, *what comes first in a sentence*.

Nominalisation also helps to condense text, as can be seen in the following example where the original sentence is tightened. It also becomes possible to add new information.

> Original: *Students should be advised to <u>avoid</u> plagiarism, which may incur penalties. The next preparatory sessions will discuss this issue.*
> Nominalised version: *<u>Avoidance</u> of plagiarism and its penalties will be discussed in the next preparatory writing sessions.* Two sentences have thus been combined.

In academic writing, the use of an abstract noun (*comparison*) in place of its verb form (*compare; compared*) can make writing more impersonal and condensed. It would be difficult for beginning writers to attempt this sort of construction in first drafts, but it is useful in later drafts to try to tighten a string of sentences, particularly with a limited word count. To move towards a more formal level may take several attempts; it is wise to remember your reader and not over-do it by becoming unnecessarily convoluted. Clarity must be the goal!

tentative tone

Frequently academic writing is tentative rather than definite in its claims. For example, contrast the following sentences and decide which seems more 'academic':

1. *Plagiarism is caused by laziness.*
2. *Laziness <u>may be</u> a contributing factor in <u>some</u> cases of plagiarism.*

The second sentence allows or concedes that there may be other causes and that plagiarism is a complex area that needs to be analysed. Sentence 1 is an example of a sweeping, all-inclusive statement that can be easily challenged: all plagiarism? every instance? Laziness is the only factor? Such a statement sounds judgemental and final. It is better to avoid using *all* or *every* unless you have considerable evidence for a claim.

Words which convey tentativeness: *may, might, should, could, probably, possibly, in some instances* and so on.

academic debate vs everyday argument

In academic writing, depending on the discipline area and the context, the tentative tone is used to suggest rather than declare, particularly in a discussion of an issue. This leaves the door open for further discussion and research, not shutting down the debate in a final and perhaps simplistic manner.

getting the balance

tightening text – try this in the final draft

The result of trying these techniques for academic writing should be a more succinct text with a concentration of information and ideas, expressed in a more formal and authoritative tone. For example, the following string of six simple texts can be tightened to show the relationship between the chunks of meaning more concisely, making every word count. Notice that each original text contains one idea or chunk of meaning.

1. *You should view the writing process as a series of drafts*
2. *that move closer towards the final version*
3. *that gets handed in.*
4. *This view of the writing process can help you to overcome writer's block.*
5. *This term refers to the experience of finding it difficult to begin writing*
6. *and it may even be impossible to begin writing.*

A more 'academic' version follows, using some of the above features of distanced writing:

> *Writer's block, which refers to the difficulty, even impossibility of beginning to write, can be overcome by viewing the assignment writing process as a series of drafts that move closer towards the final version.*

The message is now contained in one sentence, containing the main message from sentences 1 and 4. You can see how some original texts have been minimised to become phrases; the number of verbs (underlined) or events has been reduced. Abstract nouns have been used (*difficulty, impossibility*) and a passive construction (*writer's block can be overcome*) impersonalises the message (*you* has disappeared).

There is a fine balance, of course. **Too much** information in a sentence makes it reader-unfriendly by taxing the reader's short-term memory. It may also become difficult for the reader if the subject of your sentence is separated from its verb by too many extra chunks. You may make grammatical errors if you forget to make the subject, verb and pronouns match in number as demonstrated in Part 8: *agreement of subject and verb*.

Careful proofreading for a clear message is essential.

combining personal and distanced writing

Many assignments require you to switch from personal writing to impersonal writing within one text. For example, in a case study of your experience, part of your text would be a description and explanation of what happened to you, and what you observed. This means you would write from your personal perspective (see above). However the second part of the task may require you to explain your experience in relation to theories you have studied. In this part of the text it would be expected that you would move into a more formal explanation of those theories, that is, that you try to analyse your experience from an academic distance (see above).

For example: a hypothetical task
Based on your first week's experience in the university, write a report to describe how you adapted to different learning experiences in lectures and tutorials. Evaluate this experience in the light of at least three theories of learning in the university context.

Note that this task requires a comparison of experience (first part of the task) and theory (second part of the task). See Part 6: *the case study* where this task is developed in more detail.

objectivity?

While writing in a distant and formal tone is valued in much academic writing, the values and assumptions of even the most skilful writers can nevertheless be discerned through the structure of their sentences, by what is chosen as the focus of the sentence, for example. A text could be written in a number of alternative ways because a writer's choices reflect his/her viewpoint, even when the writing seems quite objective and 'sounds academic'.

Value-laden words also frequently reveal a writer's bias, without the explicit identification of a personal point of view. When you describe the *strengths* or *limitations* of a position, your judgement, even your bias is clear. You can elect to make this stronger if you describe the *valuable or useful* suggestions of one theory, or the *shortcomings and gaps* in another. Other terms such as *clearly* or *obviously*, *must* or *should* also show the writer's viewpoint.

It can be difficult to find a balance between the scholarly writing often expected in the academy and the Plain English advocated for writing for the general public. *The Style manual for authors, editors and printers* (2002) has an excellent section explaining Plain English. If a technical term is warranted in a predominantly non-technical text, a brief explanation and sometimes an example will ensure clarity, which must be your goal. At all costs avoid using emotive terms and exclamations which properly belong in advertising or propaganda. For example: *The number of students who ignore this advice is appalling!*

'Insider' language is how professionals communicate with each other – saving space in written texts and time in spoken. But it is apt to make those not in that field feel like outsiders, which is uncomfortable!

in summary

There is an old adage that you learn to write by reading. This is certainly appropriate in learning to gauge tone. Reading models of successful writing in your field such as journal articles and reports gives you the sense of its professional discourse, with all its variants. There may be a range of text types expected in your course of study, just as in the workplace, and part of your learning diverse subjects is an awareness of how to write about them. Having the skill to change your writing to suit a task is essential; being conscious of your purpose and intended audience is a very important component of such skills.

6.

academic writing is . . .
text types

the abstract and the executive summary
the annotated bibliography
the case study
the critique (critical evaluation, critical analysis)
the literature review
the reflective journal
the research review

Academic writing covers a range of text types, or genres. Each type of text has a particular purpose and audience in mind, and the assignment often reflects the texts in a particular academic field. Be aware that as circumstances change, genres may also change. Therefore, the explanations that follow offer general advice and examples; as recommended throughout this book, you should refer to specific assignment instructions and your faculty or university guidelines.

the abstract and the executive summary

the abstract

purpose and audience

Most research articles and reports are prefaced by an abstract, which is an overview or summary of the entire text. In general, this part of a report needs to be seen as an independent and separate text in its own right. Unlike other types of academic writing where paragraphing develops an idea and details elaborate it, an abstract is a short, half to one page summary where **each sentence is new information** so that a concise overview is achieved without paragraphing. The following suggestions on writing an abstract are also applicable if you have been asked to write an abstract for your essay (sometimes called a synopsis).

synopsis

Check with real models from your field of study such as research articles in journals or business reports from industry to find out how abstracts are written in your discipline. Many professional journals may post abstracts online, rather than an entire article, and these are useful both for narrowing your research, and as models of text-types. You will notice that some are written more personally than others; for example *In this article I begin by defining ...* so check your faculty's preferences and if in doubt, keep to an impersonal tone (see Part 5).

the structure of an abstract

Unlike the introduction to the report, which is the lead-in paragraph/s, the abstract or executive summary is a **text about a text**. It is usually written impersonally and could have been written by someone other than the writer. It provides a commentary on the text that follows, from its beginning to its end, so check that your abstract has at least one sentence about each section of the report (aim, method, findings, discussion, conclusion and recommendations), and in the same order. Use signal words that relate to this sequence, such as *This study is aimed ... ; This report focuses on ... ; This report begins by ... ; This study found ... ; It concludes ... ; It recommends ...* (see example below: note the underlined words which structure the abstract).

an example:
aim →
literature review →

method →
analysis →

findings →

Example: <u>This study focuses on</u> the important area of students' success in their first year in an Australian city university. <u>Drawing on</u> recent Australian research, <u>it examined</u> the effect of positive or negative feedback on students' first written assignments as motivation for continuing their studies. Samples of the student population from all faculty areas <u>were surveyed</u> and a focus group <u>was interviewed</u> about their writing at three stages of their first year experience. <u>Analysis</u> of survey and interview data indicated that students' difficulties centred on interpreting tasks and writing at an acceptable academic level. <u>It was found</u> that students who received excessive negative feedback

conclusion and → considered withdrawing from their courses, and a small percentage did not complete the
recommendation → year. <u>From this study it is concluded</u> that more attention should be given to the nature
and amount of feedback on students' written assignments, and that <u>more research is
needed</u> into students' understanding of academic writing practices.

executive summary

Some assignments, particularly in business or related subjects, may require an Executive Summary, so named from the business practice of giving executives a concise outline of the main points in the report, indicating where in the report to locate more detailed information. The summary may be several pages for a long report, and it may include headings and dot points or numbered points.

It must be concise and without details, providing a commentary on the main points (the issue or problem; objectives; methods and sources of data; findings; conclusions; any recommendations) and follow the sequence of the report itself. You should read business reports from corporations, government departments or industry for a variety of authentic models. Like the abstract, the executive summary should be written after the report has been written, when you have an overview of the whole text, and should be placed on the first pages of the report.

the annotated bibliography

*bibliography:
a list of texts
annotated:
notes made on
each text*

An annotated bibliography may be set as a separate task, for example, *Write an annotated bibliography of fifteen recent texts in the area of ...* or it may be part of a report. This task indicates to the reader that you have researched and read a sufficient number of texts on a topic that may have been set, or of your own choosing. You may have been given a reading list of books, chapters, journal articles and Internet material, or you may be searching independently for material on a topic.

*purpose and
audience* }

It will help if you imagine that the reader has not read the text and that you are giving a concise overview of it, for the purpose of using it to investigate an issue. For example, if you are researching *Factors contributing to success in university studies*, you would need to know what significant findings have already been made, by whom and for whom, and how recent these findings might be. You may also need to research general texts that discuss the issues of attrition rates in universities and what has been done to meet the problem, both in Australian universities and overseas. The key is to remember to consider the **relevance** of the text to your area of concern: Is it recent? Is it applicable? Is it useful?

the structure of an annotated bibliography

Begin the bibliography by writing the full bibliographic details of the text according to your faculty's preferred referencing system, being sure to include full author details and title, edition (if relevant), publisher and place of publication. Check guidelines for the preferred conventions for referencing electronic texts. Present your bibliography in alphabetical order. For example:

    Bloggs, J 2005, *Understanding the writing process*, Saints Press, Sydney.

There are usually two parts: a **summary** and a **critique**.

Summary: Retell the main points, identifying the particular theoretical or political perspective on which it is based. Be concise. For example:
> *This recent text takes a psycholinguistic view of the writing process, describing the stages through which an individual moves in gaining control of a variety of genres. Evidence from extensive research with students learning to write for academic purposes is presented in anecdotal examples which add interest to the theoretical explanations.*

Critique: Evaluate briefly. This is not intended to be a lengthy, critical, in-depth review about the text – that would involve a comparison with other texts, and would then become a literature review. It should give concise comments on the text and the following questions are intended as a guide:

see: literature review

» Who is the intended audience for this text – the new researcher, the expert, the general public, etc.? Would it be easy for that reader to access the information?
» Is it useful and relevant for this topic? How recent is the information?
» On what assumptions is it based? What theories does it rely on? Does it have a particular bias?

For example:
> *This is an easy-to-read text describing the writing process, which is clearly formatted for the new student; however by not including more recent theories of academic discourse that contest many of its claims, it offers a limited view of the process.*

The full annotated bibliography follows:
> Bloggs, J 2005, *Understanding the writing process*, Saints Press, Sydney.
> *This recent text takes a psycholinguistic view of the writing process, describing the stages through which an individual moves in gaining control of a variety of genres. Evidence from extensive research with students learning to write for academic purposes is presented in anecdotal examples which add interest to the theoretical explanations.*

an example

> *This is an easy-to-read text describing the writing process, which is clearly formatted for the new student; however by not including more recent theories of academic discourse that contest many of its claims, it offers a limited view of the process.*

the case study

purpose and audience

The purpose of setting a case study as an assignment is generally for you to integrate practice and theory. You may be asked to examine **a case**, that is, an event, a happening, a person or group of people, an object, a text, an idea, an institution and so on. It may be that you examine a problem or issue that has arisen in practice and analyse possible solutions that may be offered by theories.

Events may be from the past (e.g. the invention of printing) so that you write an 'historical' case study based on reading research and perhaps interviews, or your task may be more personally involving: to observe, ask questions and gather information in a field of practice or scenario (e.g. in a school, on a hospital ward, in a business office, on an engineering site)

the structure of a case study will depend on the nature of the task: e.g. a discussion essay, a comparison essay or a report

see: discussion

see Part 4: writing the report

see: levels of academic writing

an example

and to relate your data to the **models and explanations** being discussed in lectures and seminars.

In a sense, you are **analysing** 'the case', a specific instance, by mapping it against a theoretical explanation in order to understand the wider picture. You may also be asked to **evaluate** the theory or model to decide if it offers a useful explanation of the specific instance you have researched or experienced. You may be required to write an essay, where a discussion of the issues arising from the scenario is expected. Alternatively you may be required to write the assignment as a report, in which case you can use headings and subheadings to signal the structure.

If the case study centres on your own experience, your text may move from elements of personal writing or narrative as you describe the experience (giving the concrete details) to more distanced writing as you apply the theoretical explanations to it. Usually it is your analysis that is more significant than a narrative of events, but of course a narrative is easier to write! Be sure to allocate your time and words to that part of the task that shows your understanding of a theory or model and your ability to relate it to your 'case'. Note the task's instructions (*describe, evaluate*) and the text type required (*a report*).

> *Based on your first week's experience in the university, write a report to describe the different learning experiences in lectures and tutorials. Evaluate this experience in the light of at least two theories of effective learning in the university context.*

In organising your response, it may be useful to draw up a time-line of the experience, listing significant moments. Against this list, note where an experience might be related to the theories in a comparison table or grid. See Part 3: *writing a comparison*. For example:

First week's experience in the university	Theory A Bloggs 2007	Theory B Smith & Jones 2008	Evaluation based on the comparison of explanations
1. First learning experience: introductory mass lecture **in paragraph 1** (see below)	Common general anxiety – new culture **in paragraph 2** (see below)	Anxiety as inhibitor to learning (p. 45) **in paragraph 2** (see below)	*Important for orientation or a student may lose material of first lecture* **in paragraph 2** (see below)
2. Next learning experience: small group tutorial	How this theory explains the learning in this context	How this theory explains the learning in this context	*From this comparison, the most relevant explanation of my learning in this context is ...*
3. Informal discussion with other students after seminar	How this theory explains the learning in this context	How this theory explains the learning in this context	*From this comparison, the most relevant explanation of my learning in this context is ...*

And so on towards a conclusion that states which theory, or parts of theories, most usefully provide an understanding of effective learning in these contexts. A paragraph in the body of the case study about the experience may sound like this:

describing:
→ *past tense*
→ *personal perspective*
→ *concrete terms for events*

<u>My first week in university felt quite confusing as there were so many people and it was difficult to find my way around.</u> The first lecture was a new experience for me as it was very crowded and I was late because I had got lost. I sat near the back of the hall and had trouble hearing everything the lecturer said, and I began to wonder if I was going to enjoy the experience. (see paragraph 1 in grid)

Note that to write about the reality, that is, what actually happened, requires the past tense and concrete details (who, what, where, when, how) of the incident/s.

Now the next paragraph moves into the present tense to comment on the experience from a consideration of the learning theories specified in the instructions for the assignment. How does a theory explain the events? Use the present tense and generalised terms so that wider conclusions can be drawn, that is, beyond the one instance that has been described.

analysing
→ *present tense*
→ *wider perspective*
→ *abstract terms and concepts*

<u>Research (Bloggs 2007) shows this experience is common to many first year students, stemming from a general anxiety on entering a new culture.</u> This anxiety has been demonstrated to be a significant 'inhibitor' to learning (Smith & Jones 2008, p. 45), and much of the material in the first lecture may be lost if anxiety is not addressed. It is therefore important that an orientation to the culture is provided to minimise anxiety, and enable students to begin their learning from the first experience. (see paragraph 2 in grid)

As you switch from writing from the personal experience to more formal language for analysis and comparison, be sure to provide topic sentences (underlined in the above examples) and signals that indicate the stage of the text, and the connections between the parts.

For example, in the two paragraphs above, you can see how the planning grid helped to organise the material. Paragraphs were written following this grid. The topic sentences in the paragraphs indicate the purpose of each paragraph and how they are connected. In paragraph 2, *this experience* provides a cohesive link to the first paragraph. The signal *therefore* indicates an evaluation or conclusion drawn by the writer on the basis of examining experience in the light of the research and theory. In the second paragraph there are examples of paraphrasing and direct quoting with in-text citations as the writer relies on the findings of research to make a point.

see Part 1: being critical

see Part 7

Always check the focus of the case study, that is, why are you analysing this particular case? What does it demonstrate or reveal about the bigger picture? This will help you decide **the balance** between descriptions and analysis.

the critique (critical evaluation, critical analysis)

This academic task is focused on critical analysis and evaluation; it may be of a text or texts, a practice, a theory or an approach, even a person. For example:

1. Critique current policies regarding the teaching of writing in Australia.
2. Write a critical evaluation of three different approaches to teaching writing in the university context.
3. Critically analyse your own writing practices based on Bloggs' concept of metacognition.

comparison signals }

To prepare a critique it is useful to use a comparison table or grid and to use comparison and contrast signals (see Part 3: *writing a comparison*). Your purpose is to briefly highlight the main features of the material to be critiqued as in a description (the how, what and/or the who), and to then ask critical questions about that material (the why and the so what). These areas are covered in detail in Part 3: *the discussion essay – critical analysis and critical evaluation*.

Literature
in an academic sense refers to print and electronic material published on a subject, such as books, chapters from edited books and journal articles.
A review of literature
means giving an outline of the main ideas or points of one text and critically comparing and contrasting it with others on the topic or in the area.

the literature review

The purpose of writing a literature review (sometimes called a critical review) is to demonstrate that you have read widely on a topic or issue and that you have critically evaluated each text in the light of the others. It may be significant to note the difference between a primary source, which is the original text, and a secondary source which is a text telling about the original one. For example, Piaget's (1926) theories on child development are explained in his texts, the primary source. Many writers have subsequently quoted or paraphrased his theories, or relied on his findings to make their own claims,

see: primary and secondary sources }

and so these are called secondary sources. For authenticity it is better to use primary sources wherever possible.

A literature review may be a part of a larger assignment such as a report, where you provide a survey and analysis of what is known in the field on your topic, within reasonable bounds. If you are conducting your own research, it makes sense to try to find out what information or ideas already exist on which you can build. In a discussion essay or paper, a review of what is already written on the topic provides a context for your analysis of an issue, and a contrast of points of view on which to base your thesis. You may be able to comment on reasons for differences or changes in points of view.

Obviously, how many texts you include in your literature review will depend on your purpose, the assignment's parameters such as word count and time allocated, and any list of texts that may be set by the lecturer. If you are researching your own topic, it would be strategic to try to limit the scope of your investigation as much as possible in order to review a manageable number of texts. Be guided by your lecturer's advice in this regard, and confine your literature search to relevant and usually recent writers (unless an historical context is required).

Writing the literature review draws on comparison and discussion strategies, and you should read Part 3. Be careful that your summary of the text is concise, providing enough information about the text as a basis for your review. Indicate the theoretical or political perspective of the text if that is relevant as it may influence your critique. In a literature review it is common to compare and contrast the views of the writers and you may find one writer or group with whom you agree, or it may be that you only find parts of their argument reasonable. Try to look beneath the surface of the evidence or argument for assumptions – that is, what is taken for granted. Read Part 1: *being critical* for questions to pose. A useful strategy for preparing a literature review follows.

analyse each text

analysis and synthesis

» find its thesis (often found in the first and last paragraphs) and the main points on which it relies (often found in topic sentences in paragraphs). Is its purpose clear?
» check its evidence and examples: do they logically support the main thesis? Is there sufficient evidence for the claims that are made? Is there anything left out or does it have useful or challenging new insights?

synthesise your findings

» bring together your findings on each text to establish areas for comparison (a comparison table or grid is useful here)
» explain each area of similarity with examples. Useful terms and signals include: *There is consensus/agreement ... ; the writers agree ... ; commonalities include ...*

signal words

» explain each area of difference with examples. Useful terms include: *on the one hand ... ; on the other ... ; while ... ; despite ... ; however ... ; yet ... ; nevertheless ...*

the structure of a literature review

context

Like the discussion essay, your **introductory paragraph** needs to set the context and preview your thesis, that is, make a statement about your overall finding. It would be unlikely that you would read a range of texts that entirely agree or disagree with each other; it is more likely that your analysis has shown up 'grey' areas. The introduction would thus explain your own thesis about the level of agreement and the significant areas of disagreement (or vice versa). For example, three hypothetical previews follow:

1. *Bloggs (2007) and Jones (2008) have much in common with regard to ...* **(mostly agree)**
2. *Analysis of the theories of Bloggs (2007) and Smith and Jones (2008) indicates that there is little consensus ...* **(mostly disagree)**
3. *Although Bloggs (2007) and Smith and Jones (2008) may agree about ... however there are significant differences in their views on ...* **(conceding)**

see Part 5

Note that what you place first in the sentence indicates your focus: in sentence 1 above, the writers take the focus while in sentence 2 the term *analysis* moves the writing immediately into the abstract.

The **body of the review** would then need to work logically, paragraph by paragraph, through each area of similarity and difference, giving examples and acknowledging sources, and reminding the reader of the overall thesis of the essay. An example of a paragraph from the body of a literature review follows. Note the comparison of the theorists' points of view as well as the writer's own view to conclude the paragraph:

topic sentence

signals

thesis

From an analysis of both writers, a significant difference emerges regarding a definition of 'good' academic writing. <u>On the one hand</u> Bloggs (2007) describes good writing as that which obeys the academic conventions of the disciplines, is grammatically sound and well sourced, <u>while</u> Smith and Jones (2008, p. 67) regard such matters as 'niceties'. They look <u>instead</u> for evidence of an opinion in the writer, even one that challenges the established view and pushes the discipline's boundaries. The difficulty here comes from the use of the word 'good' which carries a moral connotation of well-behaved, when what should really be discussed are the skills and *abilities of students to achieve a thought-provoking text that also has those surface qualities mentioned by Bloggs (2007), qualities that seem to be mentioned only when they are missing from a text.*

see Part 3 } The **conclusion of a literature review** should reiterate the thesis, balancing the general areas of similarity and difference and commenting perhaps on the significance of the issues.

the reflective journal

This type of text may be required in order for you to map the progress and possible changes in your thinking about a subject or a topic, or about the actual learning in which you are engaged. You may be expected to make regular entries in your journal and these may be assessed by your tutor in some cases. In others you may be instructed to use your reflections built up over a period as the basis for an essay or report. For example, two hypothetical tasks:

1. *Keep a weekly journal of your reflections on your learning in this subject. Include your feelings, both positive and negative as the semester progresses, and try to explain why you feel this way at this time. What learning experiences are positive for you? What are negative? Why? Your tutor will view your journal at regular intervals throughout semester, and you will use your journal as the basis for discussion in tutorials in weeks 6 and 12.*
2. *Keep a daily journal of your experiences during the two weeks of your practical experience. In particular record notes of your interpersonal interactions with clients and reflect on how effectively you communicated with them. Give examples of some interactions that were successful and some that were not. This journal will be the basis of a reflective essay about communicative skills, related to theories discussed in lectures.*

purpose and audience } You therefore need to know both the purpose and audience for your journal writing. If the journal itself is to be assessed (example 1), you should be conscious of your reader, as advised throughout this book. Even though it will have the features of personal writing, as described in Part 5, if the reader is to make sense of it, you need to have a structure that can be followed, and clear expression. If the writing is entirely for yourself to use at a later date (example 2), you need not feel these constraints, as long as your text will make sense to you months later!

In a reflective journal you may find it easier to begin if you write in narratives, that is, stories of your experience. On reading through what happened in a given situation, you could then analyse the experience by asking some of the following questions:

the events: What happened? How did that happen? Why did that happen?
me: What do I think about it now? How does it relate to other things that I know about?
the subject being studied: How does it relate to what I am reading and learning? Have I changed how I think about this situation? What questions do I have? Where do I go from here?

If you have been given specific questions to answer or tasks to perform, for example, during your practical experience, use these as headings to help organise your responses. In this way you will be able to locate information later from your journal if you have to write an assignment, such as a report or a discussion essay. Margin notes can help highlight significant parts of your text.

the research review

ask:
→ *who?*
→ *what?*
→ *where?*
→ *when?*
→ *why?*
→ *how?*
→ *so what?*

Writing a research review is often a task for students in later years of their course, although a beginning writer may wish to use a research article in the compilation of an annotated bibliography or as part of a literature review of an issue. The research article may be data-based requiring you to analyse the research findings, or it may be based on conceptual literature. Some research articles contain both data and a literature review to be analysed.

Your task in evaluating research articles will depend very much on what the lecturer has explained in lectures about research methodologies. Usually a set of questions will have been posed about the research you are examining to enable you to critique the research design, and some questions follow to get you started. See also Part 1: *being critical*.

» What assumptions is the writer making about the issue?
» How large or small is the sample size on which discussion is based?
» How valid and reliable are the findings of the research? Examine the statistical processes. If you envisage replicating this research, can you see any problems with the methods that were followed?
» Are there any gaps in the evidence – has anything been left out?
» How has the writer supported the choice of method/procedure? Check the literature review that the article may contain and scan its reference list to check what other writers and research this article depends on. How current are the references?

Having asked the **who, what, where, when, why** and **how** questions about the research, a significant question should be discussed: **so what?** In other words, what is the significance and possible implication of the findings of this research? What may be the outcome? Who will be affected? What should happen as a result? What should be the follow-up? Frequently a finding may be that 'more research is needed' to gain a clearer picture of the issue.

It may be difficult for the beginning researcher to ask questions that imply an overview of the field. You may find your lecture notes give you guidance, and by reading what others have written about the topic, you may be able to draw comparisons. In particular, read the Discussion section of research articles carefully as it is here that the writer draws the research together to comment on what the findings mean. As with all the previous advice on text types, read similar texts in your field as models and keep in mind the two essential questions: who is my audience and what is the purpose of this text?

7.

academic writing is . . .
referencing

why reference?
what to reference
how to reference
   in-text citations
   footnote or endnote citations
   primary & secondary sources
   online sources
paraphrasing
giving direct quotes
integrating evidence
avoiding plagiarism
compiling a reference list and bibliography

Referencing frequently causes headaches for students new to the process of citation who ask:

» Why do I have to use references?
» What needs to be referenced and what does not?
» How do I do it?
» What is the difference between a reference list and a bibliography?
» Why does the punctuation matter?

what is this book's position regarding referencing?

see Part 1: understanding what is expected

It is not within the scope of this section to provide a detailed guide to all citation systems that may be used in a university setting. The intention here is to answer the questions above, explaining the processes involved, and to offer suggestions to make it easier for new academic writers. Advice regarding the **why**, **what** and **how** of referencing applies to all print and digital texts. Try not to let the task assume greater proportions; it is a matter of diligent and honest attention to detail. Your principal concern is to write clearly and to avoid plagiarism, for ethical as well as practical considerations (see below: *avoiding plagiarism*).

Specific Faculty Referencing Guidelines should be consulted for information about the conventions of sequencing, punctuating and formatting citations within texts and reference lists and bibliographies. Many faculties and universities provide these online; if yours does not, ask your tutor who may direct you to websites for other Australian or overseas universities. You should print a copy to keep at hand when proofreading. Guidelines are based on a particular Style Manual, some of which are available online. However a manual is lengthy and you will not encounter all the examples it enumerates. If you have a rather obscure problem to reference, ask your librarian to help you to access the appropriate manual or inquire at the university's learning centre. Check the edition you are using as changes may occur over time, particularly regarding punctuation. Additionally, the use of legal or legislative material requires specific conventions, as do some fields of science and business. Understanding and efficiently using these conventions is part of your induction into your field of expertise.

A faculty's preference for a particular referencing system usually relates to the writing that is published in their field; students are learning how to 'read' professional journals and research papers and to write appropriately for their discipline. Changes resulting from global influences and technology mean changes to conventions and style manuals; be sure to use the most recent editions. Differences between particular referencing systems can be mind-numbingly frustrating for students moving from one discipline or university to another (commas or full-stops? commas or no commas?), so that the best advice is to have your current Faculty Referencing Guidelines at your elbow in the final stages of making the assignment reader-ready.

why use the AGPS style? see: summary, Part 7

Examples in this book use the *Style manual for authors, editors and printers, 6th edition* (2002) which is an Australia-wide system. Sample texts given throughout this book are italicised to distinguish them from the commentary text; however in your own academic writing, use quote marks only, unless specified otherwise.

referencing

Be consistent and accurate. The punctuation details do matter. Keep in mind the reader whose focus on your work will be interrupted by inconsistent or careless referencing. It may cost you marks. Readers should be able to access your sources for themselves without a problem, so all pertinent information is required.

It may help to separate the **why** and **what** of referencing from the **how**.

why reference?

Citing information or assertions from something you have read is an important part of academic writing for several reasons:
- » You are acknowledging or giving credit to the work of someone else.
- » You are demonstrating what ideas or information you have gleaned from someone else's research or theorising as distinct from your own ideas.
- » You are demonstrating that you have researched the area so that your writing is not 'off the top of your head'.
- » You are enlisting the support of someone's research or theorising to support your own ideas or contentions.

academic debate vs everyday argument

All these factors enable the process of academic debate or argument to occur. This is in contrast to debate or argument in an everyday situation; people may have a difference of opinion or have strong views on an issue, and rely on experience (their own, or someone they know, or the radio commentator) for support. In relying on research for support, however, you are widening the argument as each researcher to whom you refer will have in turn referred to the research of others, and so on. If there are conflicts of views on an issue, it becomes even more interesting to widen the base of information and theorising on which you rely.

see also Part 5: tentative tone, passive construction

Therefore, if you rely on someone else's research or theorising – their facts and figures, their arguments and reasoning and their evidence – you need to acknowledge it. This process makes transparent the sources of your information; at the same time it demonstrates that you have done the reading expected by your lecturer or tutor.

what to reference: if you use it, reference it!

Acknowledgement applies to all sources of information, print or digital: books, chapters in books, a passing reference to another writer in a book (see below), journals, reports, databases, conference papers, dissertations and theses, brochures and newspapers. Laws, legislation, music, poetry, plays, film, videos, audio tapes, anything obtained from electronic media (CD-ROM, blogs, e-mails, etc.) and personal communications (interviews, conversations, letters, faxes) should all be acknowledged in the text if they are used in your assignment. Facts that are accepted as common knowledge (such as there are 24 hours in a day) need not be sourced, unless you are bringing them into question. Details for writing citations according to specific referencing systems are contained in Faculty Referencing Guidelines. See below for general comments and strategies.

how to reference

detail, detail, detail!

see: compiling a reference list and bibliography

see: plagiarism

see: cohesion

When making notes either on paper or cutting and pasting on computer, make certain as you read and research that you note down all the necessary bibliographic information, or use electronic software, such as *RefWorks* and *EndNote* to assist you to compile a reference list as you proceed. Such programs are not infallible however; see below.

Note page numbers with any direct quote that you copy and make sure you have the exact wording. You are less likely to lose or overlook a source and it will save you a lot of time at a later stage – many of us are familiar with the drama of trying to find page numbers or details long after we have finished with the original text. If you are cutting and pasting parts of a text as you research, be very careful to note each source. If you combine these parts later with your own writing, you may overlook a source, and so plagiarise inadvertently. Of course if you do this deliberately there are penalties. There is also the problem of writing a fragmented text that lacks a cohesive structure, as you can only see part of the text on screen and may not notice overall patchiness.

The date that you use is the copyright date, located in the first pages of a text. Do not use reprint dates, and if there are several editions, refer to the latest one as there may be significant differences between early and later editions. For e-material, be sure to also note the date on which you accessed the information, as texts online may be later modified, even removed (for further details see referencing online sources below).

primary and secondary sources

As you read, you need to be aware of the difference between a primary source and a secondary source; you will need details of both. For example, Piaget's (1926) theories on child development are explained in his texts. Many writers have subsequently quoted or paraphrased his theories, or relied on his findings to make their own claims. Be clear who it is that you are referring to: the original writer or someone writing about them. Generally it is preferred that you cite the primary source where possible. How to write a citation for a secondary source is explained below.

There are two basic methods of **referencing:** the in-text method and the footnote/endnote method. **The aim of both is to acknowledge the source accurately but in an unobtrusive manner.**

in-text citations:

are those which provide author-date-page information within the body of the text, as an indication of the source of the information and as a signal that full bibliographic detail will be given in the reference list at the end of the assignment. For an online source without page numbers, give the paragraph (or the closest previous heading). It is conventional to write the citation (that is, acknowledge the source) as closely as possible to the assertion or information. For example:

> *Students should always acknowledge the source of all information in order to avoid 'charges of cheating' (Bloggs 2007, p. 32).*

Students should always acknowledge the source of all information in order to avoid 'charges of cheating' (Bloggs 2007, para. 6). Or use *(Bloggs 2007, ¶ 6),* or *(Bloggs 2007, Cheating, para. 2).*

Full information of this source is then provided in the reference list at the end of the essay or report (for more detail see below, *compiling a reference list and bibliography*). If you are using several authors to support your view or information, write them in alphabetical order (unless your Faculty Referencing Guidelines indicate otherwise).

Acknowledgement of sources may be done in several ways using the in-text method, by paraphrasing or giving direct quotations:

see: paraphrasing

1. Using your own words to interpret and summarise, and acknowledging the source as a support for your contention. This is called indirect referencing/quoting or paraphrasing (for strategies, see paraphrasing below). For example:
Recent research (Bloggs 2007; Smith & Jones 2008) has indicated that when students understand the purpose of their assignments, their writing becomes clearer and more logically developed.

see: giving direct quotes

2. Using someone else's words as well as your own. This is called giving direct quotes or citations. For example:
Smith and Jones (2008, p. 76) have also emphasised the connection between 'metacognition and clarity of argument'.

footnote or endnote citations:

are preferred by some faculties. For paraphrases or direct quotes, a superscript number is used to indicate that there are more details about the text at the foot of the page or at the end of the chapter or text. For example:
Recent research[1] has indicated that when students understand the purpose of their assignments, their writing becomes clearer and more logically developed. Smith and Jones have also emphasised the connection between 'metacognition and clarity of argument'[2].

At the foot of the page or at the end of the chapter:
1. J Bloggs 2007, *Understanding the reading process*, Saints Press, Sydney.
2. P Smith & M Jones 2008, *Improving university students' writing*, Blah Press, New York, p. 76.

There would also be an alphabetical list of all sources at the end of the text as a reference list or bibliography (see below).

Footnotes may become too lengthy so it may be better to use the endnote system. In some instances, an in-text citation system may also use endnotes to contain extra information or comments that would otherwise 'clutter' the text. To avoid repetitions of the same reference, there are conventions using Latin phrases in footnotes such as *ibid.* (in the same work) and *loc. cit.* (in the place cited). Footnotes are not viable in an on-screen text, where interactive pop-up or drop-down boxes may be used instead. Again, Faculty Referencing Guidelines are essential reading to master these conventions, which are not used in all systems.

As in-text methods are more commonly used, the following examples offer a general guide only, using the AGPS (2002) author-date style. For detailed information, consult your Faculty Referencing Guidelines.

online sources

Students new to online researching will find assistance in their library, and it is best to come to terms with the technology right from the start. If necessary, book into courses that are often provided in the early weeks and use your library's online help resources. Many faculties also provide orientation to discipline-specific digital material and databases through training sessions or online guides. If you are changing disciplines, or universities (even subjects), do not assume that all conventions are the same. As suggested at the outset of this book, be prepared to ask!

Only use reputable material you can source!

Be particularly careful to find the source of any material you may wish to use from the Internet as there is much unattributed material there: it may be advertising or promotional material, someone's personal and unsubstantiated opinions or anecdotes, even crackpot theories! You should only rely on Internet material if you can source it – who wrote it, where and when? What are the credentials of the writer? Who is the publisher/producer of the text? You need to be a super-critical reader here.

In-text: referring to an online source follows the same logic as for print materials. You need to provide the reader with author, date and page (or paragraph or nearest previous heading) as closely as practicable to the idea or information being cited. For example:

> Students should always acknowledge the source of all information in order to avoid 'charges of cheating' (Bloggs 2007, para. 6). Or use (Bloggs 2007, ¶ 6) or use (Bloggs 2007, Cheating, para. 2)

The reader must then be able to access the same information from the details you provide in your reference list, so it is particularly important with e-information that in your notes you copy exactly all characters, symbols and punctuation from the original, however lengthy. Material may change with time so you need to note the date accessed (or viewed). The conventions for using electronic sources in academic writing will depend on the type of source (e.g. web page, e-mail etc.) and on your faculty's requirements. Once again, the best advice is to rely on your Faculty Referencing Guidelines as it is beyond the scope of this text to provide every example (see below: *compiling a reference list and bibliography*).

primary & secondary sources

You should clearly indicate when you are relying on a writer's interpretation of another writer.

For example: You are reading a text by Bloggs, written in 2007 and it refers to a finding by Brown in 2005. Brown is therefore the primary source. You wish to use the finding and so you must acknowledge that it is Brown's, but you must also acknowledge that you have not read Brown's text and that you are relying on Bloggs' version (the secondary source). This is called a **passing reference**, that is, Bloggs is referring to Brown in passing. The page number is given because Brown's actual words are quoted by Bloggs on page 89 and this is the text you are actually using. The citation follows:

a passing reference

> In evaluating the importance of preparation in the process of writing, it is useful to compare the grades that students receive for assignments that have been hurriedly written with those that have moved through extensive

referencing

what text is actually in front of you?

revisions. One such study (Brown, cited in Bloggs 2007, p. 89) indicates that some students are willing to 'risk poor grades rather than give up social time with their friends'.

Some faculties will accept an abbreviated citation of a secondary source, such as (*Brown in Bloggs 2007, p. 89*) so check your Faculty Referencing Guidelines. In your Reference List, you give details of the Bloggs' text, not Brown's as you have not used Brown's. A critical point emerges if there is any contention that Bloggs may have misused Brown's findings; in that case you would have to read Brown's original 2005 text.

acknowledging a chapter

When a writer has contributed a chapter to someone's text, he/she is a part-author of the text and so is a primary source. You need to cite that writer in your essay or report and give that writer a full citation in the reference list. This is like the acknowledgement you give the writer of an article in a journal volume that includes several writers. Thus if Smith has written a chapter in Bloggs' text, Smith's chapter is listed in the reference list and Bloggs as the editor is also mentioned. Note that these are in alphabetical order. For example:

Bloggs, J (ed.) 2008, *Writing in the academy*, Education Texts, Adelaide.

Smith, T 2008, 'Investigating Writer Identity', in J Bloggs (ed.), *Writing in the academy*, Education Texts, Adelaide, pp. 101-144.

Check your particular Faculty Referencing Guidelines to comply with the preferred referencing system for capitalisation, punctuation and sequencing conventions.

paraphrasing

Your paraphrase of the 'expert' is usually more valued than copying a lot of their words. Keep direct quotes of actual words to a minimum: that 'telling' word or that 'neat' definition; always acknowledge the sources of your information.

To paraphrase is to use your own words to restate the sense of your source material rather than to quote the original directly. This frequently means summarising the essence of what someone else has written. If you are paraphrasing a general idea that appears throughout the original text, it is usual to acknowledge it with the author's name and date of publication in brackets following your own words. There may be more than one source on which you rely for an assertion. For example:

Recent research (Bloggs 2007; Smith & Jones 2008) has indicated that students' writing communicates more logically if the purpose of an assignment is understood.

If your paraphrase includes **specific information** from your source, it is usual to add the page number (or paragraph number for online texts without page numbers). For example:

Three issues have been identified regarding student writing in university (Bloggs 2007, p. 16).

Three issues have been identified regarding student writing in university (Bloggs 2007, par. 6).

Generally what is valued is evidence of your reading by your use of the source material so that it supports your thesis or is part of your explanation. This shows you are interpreting what has been said, rather than copying it into your text. An essay that comprises masses of direct quotations strung together may seem more the product of cutting and pasting than the student's analysis. There is also the serious danger of plagiarism, however inadvertent, if the source drops off the page!

A strategy for paraphrasing:
→ *Acknowledge the source in your notes.*
→ *Read the original, pen-in-hand to underline key words and make margin notes on your photocopy or printout.*
→ *Close the page.*
→ *Note down the main ideas roughly and quickly.*
→ *Check with the original that you have retained the main sense of it.*
→ *Edit and proofread.*

Students sometimes find it difficult to paraphrase and find that they may be only altering one or two words. This is not sufficient as it is expected that you **interpret** the source material. If you try to do this with the original in front of you, it is easy to rely on its sentence construction and vocabulary, and in essence to plagiarise it, as in the example below where single words and word order have been changed with a minor grammatical alteration. Essentially the original remains as it was and without an acknowledgement: this is plagiarism. For example, an original source states:
  'When outlining the main points in a discussion paper, the writer needs to ensure cohesive ties logically connect the steps in the argument' (Bloggs 2007, p. 18).

An inadequate paraphrase: *Outlining the main points in a discussion paper requires the writer to ensure cohesive ties join the steps logically in the argument.*

With or without the citation, this sentence has not paraphrased the original text.

A paraphrase that indicates the source of an idea follows:
  To develop a cohesive academic argument, each point needs to be linked to the task (Bloggs 2007).

see Part 5: making it 'sound' academic

Students sometimes say that as this strategy relies on a memory of the general sense of the information, it does not 'sound as good' as the original. You can work on the language to rectify this, but your own interpretation is what the lecturer wants because in this way he/she can identify whether you really understand the material. This, after all, would be the way you would explain the material in a seminar or tutorial, relying on your memory but explaining it in your own way.

giving direct quotes

When using the actual wording of the original text, which is often effective in giving a definition or explanation (and when you really cannot find another way of expressing that idea), it is necessary to add the page number (*Bloggs 2007, p. 46*) and to include all words quoted within single quote marks (other systems use double quotes or italics). When using another writer's actual words, you should not change anything. If you need to omit some text because you just want a word or phrase, you can indicate the gap with three dots. For example:
  Bloggs' (*2007, p. 46*) finding that *'when students understand … their writing becomes clearer and more logically developed'* supports the contention that transparency is essential.

When directly quoting a segment in this way, try to make your sentence flow grammatically into the other writer's words (see below: *integrating evidence*). Remember that even if you only use one or two words from a source, you need to acknowledge it. For example:

> *Smith and Jones (2008, p. 76) have also emphasised the connection between 'metacognition and clarity of argument'.*

word count }

If you need to give a long direct quote (more than 30 words), it is usual to indent to signal that it is another text within your text, and you do not need inverted commas (see example b) next page). Usually, long or block quotes are not counted in your word count because they are not **your words**: check with your specific Faculty Referencing Guidelines or ask. To avoid confusion, if you are concerned about word length, check whether your lecturer uses a computer check (every word) or a manual count (does not include short words such as 'a, and' etc.). More importantly, if you are concerned about the length of your assignment, you need to check what you have included that may not be so relevant to the task. Check again the wording of the task and ask: Does this paragraph pass the 'paragraph test'?

see: paragraph test }

integrating evidence

Whether you are paraphrasing or quoting directly, you need to integrate the source material smoothly into your own text. There are several ways to do this:

1. You may wish to make the writers explicitly **part of your argument** or explanation as participants, in which case their names are part of your sentence and only the date (and page number for a direct quote) is placed in brackets. This is particularly useful in a comparison of writers or theorists.

see: literature review, Part 6 }

> *Bloggs (2007) has suggested that students' writing communicates more logically if the purpose of an assignment is understood. Smith and Jones (2008, p. 76) have also emphasised the connection between 'metacognition and clarity of argument'.*

2. You may wish to focus on **the issue** or your point of view, and use the sources for support. In this case, the writers' names are included in the brackets with the date (and page number for a direct quote).

see: what comes first in the sentence, Part 5 }

> *Understanding the purpose of an assignment and an awareness of structure may result in clearer, more logical communication (Bloggs 2007; Smith & Jones 2008).*

The choice to do this would depend on what you want to focus on in the sentence: the writer/researcher (sentence 1) or the issue/idea (sentence 2).

Your writing will flow more effectively if you can integrate your evidence into your sentence structure, rather than adding on a quote. Which of the following examples reads more easily?

example a)
> *Recent research (Bloggs 2007, p. 46) has indicated that 'when students understand the purpose of their assignments, their writing becomes clearer*

and more logically developed'. Subject outlines and task instructions frequently indicate the relevance of an assignment task to the course objectives.

example b)
> It is important that students read their subject outlines and task instructions in order to understand why a particular task has been set and to view it in the context of course objectives:
>> The issue of providing precise instructions is central for assessment tasks. In surveying a large group of students about their knowledge about the writing process, it was found that when students understand the purpose of their assignments, their writing becomes clearer and more logically developed.
>>
>> (Bloggs 2007, p. 46)

how many voices in the text?

In contrast to example a) above, in example b) a direct quote has been tacked onto the paragraph and tends to fragment the reading. Generally, direct quotes of 30 words or more (block quotes) should be formatted as above, indented on a new line without quotation marks and with a space before and after. You can see how it breaks the flow of the text, which is justified if it makes a significant point, but your aim should be to take the reader through your text without hiccoughs, stops and starts. Do you need a lengthy quote here? Why? Can you make the same point more succinctly in your own words? Too many direct quotes, especially if added on rather than integrated into the text, may create dissonance and irritation, and the reader 'hears' a sometimes confusing medley of different voices. It may also lead to plagiarism if excessive cutting and pasting of source materials causes the sources themselves to disappear (deliberately or not!).

color or colour? recognise or recognize?

Proofreading your citations is important for consistency. It will distract the reader if you use a variety of conventions and in some faculties marks will be deducted. Do not rely on the spell checker; it is not infallible, and usually defaults to American rather than Australian/British spelling.

When you have read your assignment several times checking for meaning and the logical development of information and ideas, check that you have supported your assertions and provided evidence for information you have used by including citations. For every claim you have made, ask 'Who says so?' 'In whose opinion?' because these are the questions that the reader may also ask. Now turn your attention to the smallest details of formatting to ensure that you are following the required conventions for your particular referencing system and that there is consistency throughout your text. Often this becomes a matter of punctuation: where to put a comma, or a space and so on; it does matter to a reader who expects these mechanics to be conscientiously done.

avoiding plagiarism

If material is taken from a source without acknowledgement, it is considered plagiarism, which then is considered stealing if it seems deliberate. With the increasing use of the Internet, sources available to students have exponentially multiplied. It is therefore becoming even more important to universities to identify plagiarism; your university or faculty will make clear its policy regarding penalties for deliberate and repeated instances. Therefore you should always take careful note of any sources you have used (non-print as well as print) and be sure to include them in your text. See above: *how to reference*.

group work – whose work?

If a student copies another student's assignment it is also considered plagiarism. It may be useful for you to work with others in researching and planning an assignment and in some subjects students are expected to work in collaborative groups. However the assignment you hand in must be your own work, or if a group task, should clearly indicate which part is yours.

Lecturers are familiar with the texts you will be using and will recognise them; if you use something they do not recognise, or if they have doubts that you have correctly cited a source, it is likely that they will want to read or view it for themselves. There are also software programs in use that identify plagiarism. Your reference list should enable the reader to find and check the source easily.

compiling a reference list and bibliography

In-text and footnote/endnote citations provide a short-hand indication of the source of information which serves to direct the reader to the reference list at the end of the assignment. As with in-text referencing, be careful and consistent in formatting and punctuation. Electronic software, such as *RefWorks* and *EndNote* will assist you to compile a reference list in a range of referencing systems, but any inconsistencies in your initial input will cause problems. This task still requires patience and thoroughness.

A reference list contains all texts to which you have **specifically referred** in your assignment in your paraphrases and direct quotes. A bibliography is a list of **additional texts** that you have read for the assignment but have not specifically referred to in your assignment and should be listed separately after the reference list. Sometimes the terms bibliography and reference list are used interchangeably, so if you are in any doubt you should consult the Faculty Referencing Guidelines or ask a lecturer or tutor what they require. Usually it is in the later or postgraduate years of study that a bibliography is required, rather than in early undergraduate writing. Again, if you are in any doubt, ask! Lecturers may point you to journal articles in your field as models of how reference lists are compiled in your discipline area or a 'model assignment' may be provided.

This section gives general guidance so that you understand the reasons for all the 'rules'. Formatting details for compiling a reference list and bibliography are not given here as you will need the specific instructions provided by your Faculty Referencing Guidelines to ensure you meet the requirements of your discipline. You will need to proofread carefully for details of formatting, spacing and punctuation. All sources of information whether print or digital are alphabetically arranged together (e.g. books, chapters, online journal articles, film, etc.), at the end of the essay or report, starting on a new page, entitled **Reference List** and/or

Bibliography. Note that personal communications which cannot be verified are not included unless required by your lecturer for a specific purpose. The AGPS style is used here.

Internet sources or electronic communications: your reader must be able to locate the information or check it. You should copy exactly all characters, symbols and punctuation from the original, however lengthy. Material may change with time and should include the date accessed (see example below).

Books: reference in full giving the author, title, date, publisher, city of origin and edition (if not the first). The date that you use is the copyright date, located in the first pages of a text. Do not use reprint dates, and if there are several editions noted, refer to the latest one, that is, the text you have in front of you, as there may be significant differences between early and later editions. Note that the title is usually italicised or underlined. The AGPS style manual suggests capitalisation of the first word only in a book title; other styles capitalise the main words (but not *and, the* etc.). Proper nouns and names require capital letters. For example:

>Bloggs, J 2007, *Understanding the reading process*, Saints Press, Sydney.

Add the URL for books accessed online, giving the date accessed. Check your Faculty Referencing Guidelines for preferred conventions, such as the sequencing of date-accessed information (some include within the main citation, others put it at the end; some prefer *accessed* or *viewed*). For example:

>Bloggs, J 2008, *Understanding reading in the academic context and for professional purposes*, Saints Press, Sydney, accessed 12 June 2009, <http://reading/writingandcitingonline.com.au>.

Chapters: give the details of an edited book if you have referred to a specific chapter, as well as the details about the chapter itself, in alphabetical order of course (see: *acknowledging a chapter*). Again, check the preferred conventions for capitalising in titles (in AGPS, capitals for chapters but not for books).

>Bloggs, J (ed.) 2008, *Writing in the academy*, Education Texts, Adelaide.

>Brown, T 2008, 'Investigating Writer Identity', in J Bloggs (ed.), *Writing in the academy*, Education Texts, Adelaide, pp. 101-144.

Journal articles are located by the **volume and number of the journal** to which they belong. Journals may publish monthly, quarterly or bi-annually (or another variation); therefore it is important to include all details. Give its URL or its Document Object Identifier (DOI) and the date that you viewed it. Check your guidelines for capitalisation details (in AGPS, capitals for journal titles but not journal articles).

- name of the journal, usually italicised or underlined (e.g. *Australian Journal of Writing and Citing*)
- exact date (e.g. *October 2008*) or season (e.g. *Spring 2008*)
- volume and number details and the page numbers of the particular article (e.g. vol. 6, no. 3, pp. 123-130) Page numbers may not be available online so use a paragraph number or the nearest previous heading. Give date viewed/accessed if online.
- URL or DOI for online journals (do not underline or hyperlink).

For example:
> Bloggs, J 2008, 'Investigating academic writing', *Australian Journal of Writing and Citing*, vol. 6, no. 3, pp. 123-130.

For an online journal article:
> Bloggs, J 2008, 'Investigating academic writing', *Australian Journal of Writing and Citing*, vol. 6, no. 3, accessed 16 March 2009, <http://www.readingwritingandcitingonline.com.au>.

summary

In summary, you will minimise stress if you pay close attention to **detail, detail, detail** as you make notes, write drafts and polish your citations and reference list. Allow sufficient time to integrate your sources and avoid cutting and pasting to excess. Remember it is **your** writing and use of research that is valued, not a compilation of other writers' words.

Acknowledge all those who have contributed to your point of view or your findings so that your assignment has honesty and integrity. The **how** of referencing is then a matter of careful and consistent mechanics, best checked and double-checked at the final proofreading stage. Be prepared to learn from your mistakes – we all make them! – and be aware that conventions change as circumstances change. The *Style manual* used in this book has been published six times and reprinted with corrections ten times, so far!

How one style guide has evolved:

AGPS is an Australian version of the Harvard style. There have been new editions (1972, 1978, 1988, 1994) since its origin with the Commonwealth Government Printing Office (1966), which later became the Australian Government Publishing Service (AGPS) (1970-1997); hence you may hear it sometimes referred to as the AGPS style. It is now a commercial publication, based on the advice of communications and publishing professionals, to include the global influence of the Internet. AGPS is used in most government, and many business publications. You may also hear of the Chicago style, another version of Harvard preferred by some. Then there are the American Psychological Association system (APA) and the Modern Language Association of America system (MLA) used by some faculties. You will no doubt find differences in writers' citation preferences in your research reading, but your academic writing should be consistent within the conventions of your subjects.

Useful guides and Style Manuals

American Psychological Association 2001, *Publication manual of the American Psychological Association*, 5th edn, Washington DC.

Bennett, TJ (ed) 2009, *Referencing guide*, 11th edn, Edith Cowan University, Mount Lawley, Western Australia, viewed 6 March 2009, <http://www.ecu.edu.au/CLT/pdf/refguide.pdf>.

Chicago manual of style: for authors, editors and copywriters 1993, 14th edn, University of Chicago Press, Chicago.

Guide to writing assignments. UTS: Business 2006, Faculty of Business, University of Technology, Sydney, viewed 6 March 2009, <http://www.business.uts.edu.au/teaching/guide/guide.pdf>.

Harvard Referencing. The 'In-Text' system n.d., Learning Centre, University of NSW, viewed 6 March 2009, <http://www.lc.unsw.edu.au/onlib/ref.html>.

Modern Language Association of America 2009, *MLA handbook for writers of research papers*, 7th edn, New York.

Style manual for authors, editors and printers 2002, 6th edn, John Wiley and Sons Australia, Milton, Queensland.

the URLs given here were accurate at the time of writing

8.

academic writing is . . .
proofreading

common sentence level problems
  incomplete sentences
  agreement of subject & verb
  consistency in use of pronouns
  pronouns & sexist language
  verb tense
  apostrophes

common misspellings and spelling strategies

In the wider community and the media generally, correct spelling, punctuation and grammar have always been taken as a sign of 'having an education' and being literate. As mentioned earlier, global influences and the explosion of information through technology are resulting in changes to some language conventions and what is considered acceptable or appropriate. However, whenever a usage is changing, there will be controversy about the whole issue of 'correctness', and about who is to determine the acceptability of new forms. Frequently the issues discussed below represent a word, spelling or grammatical form that is in a state of flux and therefore a topic of debate. To be literate today means keeping up with this debate, and the university experience should develop your confidence as a writer in your field. To that end, flexibility, attention to detail and skill in proofreading are essential.

Discussions with lecturers and tutors about students' writing frequently highlight problems with proofreading. Spelling, grammar and punctuation errors distract from the content of the assignment and it is not enough to rely on computer programs that check spelling and grammar; many default to an American spelling and some will 'correct' a grammatical expression incorrectly! As your assignment moves towards completion, be sure to plan enough time for thorough checking. Do not rush this stage of the writing process.

Sometimes reading the text aloud will pick up errors that go unnoticed in silent reading. Alternatively, ask someone else to read it, even aloud, which will also help you to notice problems of awkward expression, or changes in tense. Many writers have a particular 'glitch' or 'demon' that they need to be aware of; it may be a particular word that you commonly misspell, or a frequent typing error, or a punctuation problem that you have to remember to check each time.

There are several areas where mistakes are commonly made and a brief explanation of these follows. If you have a significant problem in these areas, you should invest in a grammar textbook which contains explanations and examples, or attend a grammar class. Several useful texts are listed at the end of this section.

common sentence level problems

incomplete sentences

Often when a writer thinks a sentence is too long, a full-stop will be dropped in. However it may in fact create sentence fragments. Ambiguity often results as the reader has to work hard to connect the fragments. You need to be sure that every sentence expresses a complete idea and that a full-stop signals the end of one idea and the beginning of the next. The example below shows how punctuation incorrectly used can cause confusion and even irritation for the reader. An incomplete sentence has been underlined.
> *Bloggs' research (2007) indicates clear links between negative feedback to students' initial academic writing and decisions to drop out in the first year of study. <u>Advocating the importance of early preparatory programs</u>. Smith and Jones (2008) argue for greater resources in this area.*

Where should the incomplete part be attached? It makes a difference in sense:

Bloggs' research (2007) indicates clear links between negative feedback to students' initial academic writing and decisions to drop out in the first year of study, advocating the importance of early preparatory programs. Smith and Jones (2008) argue for greater resources in this area.

Here the advocating belongs to Bloggs.

OR *Bloggs' research (2007) indicates clear links between negative feedback to students' initial academic writing and decisions to drop out in the first year of study. Advocating the importance of early preparatory programs, Smith and Jones (2008) argue for greater resources in this area.*

Now the advocating belongs to Smith and Jones.

Do not use a comma to make connections between different ideas, as a comma signals a pause before continuing the point. Use **a full stop to separate** into two sentences or a semi-colon if you want two ideas to be juxtaposed. If you wish to connect the two points, use a **joining word** that explicitly shows that connection. In the next example, the inappropriate comma is indicated:

Omission of a citation may incur a <u>penalty, this may</u> mean failing the assignment.

Corrected 1: *Omission of a citation may incur a <u>penalty. This may</u> mean failing the assignment.* The two ideas are separated by a full stop.

Corrected 2: *Omission of a citation may incur a <u>penalty; this may</u> mean failing the assignment.* The two ideas are juxtaposed by a semi-colon.

Corrected 3: *Omission of a citation may incur a <u>penalty which may</u> mean failing the assignment.* The two ideas are joined by a connector.

agreement of subject & verb

Agreement refers to the matching of the subject and its verb as either both singular or both plural. In a long sentence (or an overlong one), the subject of the sentence may be at a distance from its verb causing a mix-up of singulars and plurals, and exasperating the reader.

In the following example, can you detect the problems of subject-verb agreement?

The student who views the process of assignment writing as drafts that moves closer towards the final version are able to overcome writer's block.

Incorrect agreements are shown below:

singular subject – *student* → but plural verb – *are able*
plural subject – *drafts* → but singular verb – *moves*

It is easier to make everything plural:

Corrected: *<u>Students</u> who <u>view</u> the process of assignment writing as <u>drafts</u> that <u>move</u> closer towards the final version <u>are able</u> to overcome writer's block.*

Alternatively, move the verb closer to its subject:

The <u>student is able</u> to overcome writer's block by viewing the process of assignment writing as drafts that move closer towards the final version.

A semi-colon is useful; it is not such a definite pause as a full stop, but it is 'stronger' than a comma.

tutors: *3rd person*
you: *2nd person*
we: *1st person*
you: *2nd person*

consistency in use of pronouns

Pronoun use has been discussed earlier, in Part 5: *writing from a personal perspective*. Linked to problems of agreement, the pronoun references you use should not be mixed. Clarity is lost, as in the following example:

Tutors should aim to give clear explanations.[1] You should use an appropriate level of language that students understand.[2] Don't use too much jargon in early sessions.[3] We all need to remember that short and simple explanations are best so that your students understand what you want.[4]

sentence 1: in the third person: describing tutors in an impersonal way.

sentence 2: in the second person: now the writer is addressing the reader directly as 'you', assuming that the reader IS the tutor previously mentioned. The writer is telling the reader what to do.

sentence 3: in the second person again ('you' is understood) but expressed as a command to the reader. Now the text has become quite bossy!

sentence 4: in the first person, assuming the writer and reader are both tutors ('we'). This seems to be an appeal to the reader to identify with the writer. The text then reverts to the second person at the end of the sentence to refer directly to the reader again.

The use of pronouns in this example indicates that the writer is positioning the reader as a participant in the text (1st and 2nd person: 'we', 'you') making assumptions about the reader and creating a personal tone that may not be appropriate (does the reader want or expect to be told what to do, as in sentence 3?). It is also very inconsistent, indicating that the writer is unsure of his/her audience.

pronouns & sexist language

Following from inconsistencies with pronouns is the issue of gender in the use of pronouns. It is expected that your writing will be gender-inclusive. Some older texts that you may read assume, for example, that all engineers are male, and all nurses are female. Some people still do! Gender inclusiveness means using the pronouns *he/she, him/her, his/her* to agree with singular nouns such as *engineer, nurse.* If you find this awkward as a matter of style, use the plural consistently through the text: that is, *engineers, nurses > they, them, their.*

changing conventions?

There has been some debate that *they* should be used as an all-purpose pronoun (like *you*) for singular and plural, to avoid the awkward *him/her* and to facilitate reading. In many texts this is being done. When the usage (or spelling) of a word is in a state of change, you will find various reactions; some accept *they* as common usage for singulars (advocated by the AGPS in 1996, and traced back as a practice to Shakespeare on occasions). It is certainly in widespread use in spoken English. It is technically ungrammatical, however, as a pronoun should agree with, or match its noun (see above). You may therefore find that using *they / them / their* for singular references is corrected in some assignments and not in others. Wherever possible, using plural nouns (engineers, nurses) will avoid this dilemma.

verb tense

Generally, choosing past or present tense in academic writing depends on whether you are writing about something that happened at a specific time (such as an incident in a classroom, on a ward or on site) or something that is on-going (such as an idea, or a theory to explain a process). This may mean that a piece of writing moves between the past and present tense as it explains an event that occurred (past) then moves to offer an explanation of how or why it occurred (present). In the following paragraph, specific events are described in the past tense.

see: case studies

> My first week in university _felt_ quite confusing as there _were_ so many people and it _was_ difficult to find my way around. The first lecture _was_ a new experience for me as it _was_ very crowded and I _was_ late because I _had got_ _lost_. I _sat_ near the back of the hall and _had_ trouble hearing everything the lecturer _said_, and I _began_ to wonder if I _was going to enjoy_ the experience.

use timeless present tense to describe research findings

In the case of research findings or theoretical explanations, the present tense (sometimes called the **timeless or universal present tense**) is used because the discussion is on-going. For example, the next paragraph comments on the above experience from a consideration of learning theories and so uses the timeless present tense.

> Research (Bloggs 2007) _suggests_ that such an experience _is_ common to many first year students, stemming from a general anxiety on entering a new culture. This anxiety _has been demonstrated_ to be a significant 'inhibitor' to learning (Smith & Jones 2008, p. 45), and much of the material in the first lectures may be lost if anxiety _is not addressed_. It _is_ therefore important that an orientation to the culture _is provided_ to minimise anxiety, and enable students to begin their learning from the first experience.

However, as with much of the advice about academic writing, these are general observations and you need to find out the current conventions that exist in your particular field of study. Use the journals that lecturers recommend in your field as models, paying careful attention to the way that tenses are used.

apostrophes

What is it about the rogue apostrophe that is such a problem for so many writers? Notice how often misuse of the apostrophe is commented upon in the media. Some say it is a sign of the times, a lowering of literacy standards. Others claim that only punctuation pedants are bothered by its misuse, while some advocate its entire removal by legislation. It is surprising how much passion is generated by a tiny punctuation mark!

Nevertheless, it remains the case that in the wrong place, the apostrophe can turn a message into nonsense. In the interests of clarity in your writing, it should be a main concern in the proofreading process.

A basic misunderstanding seems to be that the apostrophe makes words plural. It does not. It has **two purposes**:

1. to show contractions

A contraction is where letters have been left out, marked by an apostrophe; for example: *don't* for *do not*, *won't* for *will not*, *it's* for *it is* and so on. As contractions in academic writing are often the mark of informality, creating a more conversational tone, many academics do not accept them. Nevertheless, in some academic fields there is an increasing tendency to reduce the distance between writer and audience, which makes contractions acceptable. You must be guided by current practice as reflected in journals and your faculty's own publications.

2. to show possession

An apostrophe is used to signal ownership or possession when used with nouns, and sometimes **s** is added. To sort out problems that may occur, ask 'who owns it?' The answer is called the stem or base word, or the 'owner-word'. An apostrophe is inserted **after** the owner-word. For example:

1. *The idea of the student* → *the student's idea.*
    student (singular) is the owner-word. Show ownership with **an apostrophe and s**.

owner-word + apostrophe then s if needed

2. *The idea of many students* → *many students' idea.*
    students (plural) is the owner-word. Show ownership with **an apostrophe**. The owner-word already ends with **s** so another one is not needed; you only 'hear' one **s** sound.

There is some controversy about what to do when the owner-word is someone's name that already ends with s. One view is that it is optional to add an extra s as it can be spoken that way. However as different people will pronounce names differently it is probably clearer if you always add the extra **s**. For example:

The idea of James. James is the owner-word so add the apostrophe and s → *James's idea.* You may also see it written as *James' idea* without an extra **s**.

Thus the apostrophe is always **added to** the existing owner-word (*student, students, James*) to show possession and **then** the decision is made about adding **s**. Is there already an **s**? Does it need an extra **s**? The apostrophe **should never intrude** into the owner-word as that creates ambiguity: changing a word from plural to singular, (*many student*), making a new word (*Jame*) or even nonsense.

Try these – insert the apostrophe:
1. A policys implications
2. several theorists points of view
3. Professor Bloggs followers

Answers:
1. *policy's* – owner-word is *policy*, singular. The implications of a policy.
2. *theorists'* – owner-word is *theorists*, plural. The points of view of several theorists.
3. *Bloggs's* or *Bloggs'* – owner-word is *Bloggs*. The followers of Professor Bloggs. (If you wrote Blogg's you have changed the name to Professor Blogg!).

possessive pronouns family:
my, mine
your, yours
his, her, hers, its
our, ours
their, theirs

There is one exception to the rule about adding an apostrophe to show ownership, and that is the **family of pronouns**. For example: *ours, yours, his, hers, theirs, whose*. These words already indicate possession and therefore need no punctuation to signal ownership. You would not think of inserting an apostrophe into these words (*hi's ? her's?*) so it helps to think of *its* in the same way. Thus *he owns* → *his; it owns* → *its*.

the demon:
its/it's

Beware also of the contraction *who's there?* meaning *who is*. Not to be confused with the possessive *whose book?* – no apostrophe needed.

For example:
This theory has its origin in the writer's experience ...

If an apostrophe is inserted into this example, it signals the contraction *it is* and so the sentence would in fact read: *This theory has <u>it is</u> origin in the writer's experience ...*

Try these – insert the apostrophe:
1. *Its problem is that it is confusing.*   Apostrophe? yes/no
2. *My problem is that **its** confusing.*   Apostrophe? yes/no

Answers:
1. no
2. yes

If you are not sure, always substitute **it is** for every **its/it's** in your text to check if it makes sense. You will soon hear the problem of the misplaced apostrophe. Better still, avoid the confusion by not using contractions in your text.

common misspellings and spelling strategies

Most computer spell-check programs use American spelling which may cause a problem if it is not acceptable in your faculty. Check your Faculty Referencing Guidelines, *Macquarie dictionary*, the *Australian Oxford dictionary* or the *Style manual* if it is an issue. As mentioned previously, computers and global events are changing attitudes to spelling in some areas and there are signs of some commonalities being accepted to expedite communication.

If you are troubled by spelling, keep a spelling folder or notebook just for recording frequently used words that cause concern and refer to it often. It sometimes helps to print troublesome words in large colourful letters on a poster near your desk for repeated reinforcement. The more you look at the spelling the more familiar you become with how it looks, and it removes the stress of trying to remember – often the original reason for confusion over a word is locked in!

more demons

There are some commonly confused pairs and demons which are listed here with suggestions of 'tricks' to aid recall. The list is by no means exhaustive but you can devise your own imaginative cue or trick to help you remember a troublesome word. Attacking the demon as a problem to be solved, rather than a burden to be memorised, can help you to become conscious of how the word is formed, which can also aid recall.

spelling strategies

1. relate a word to other members of the same family, for example:
   <u>defin</u>ition – <u>defin</u>ite (like <u>finite</u>)

2. remember small words inside larger ones, for example:
   <u>critic</u> in *criticise, criticism*
   ice in *practice* (nouns – the doctor's practice)
   ice in *advice* (nouns – the advice of my friend)

3. A memory cue may also help with pairs that sound alike, for example:
» *effect* (noun): Put *the* in front to indicate it is a noun: *the effect* (hear the *e* sound in th*e* and *effect* and see the double *e* – th*e effect*).
Affect is the verb: e.g. *to affect, affected by the decision*.
» *allusion* (noun): a passing reference to something, to *allude* to it, to make an *allusion* to a poem.
An *illusion* is a false impression. An optical *illusion* makes you *ill!*
» *cite* (verb): to quote, mention in support, belongs to the family of *citation*. On the other hand, *site* belongs to the family of *situation* (noun – the site, the position or location; or verb – to site, to locate something).

If you do need to memorise words, try the **Look and Say – Cover – Write – Check method**, utilising the sight and sound of the word and repetition as a learning strategy. This also works for memorising facts and figures for exams. Make sure you tackle a **short** list of words or facts at a time so that you do not overload your short-term memory. As has been explained in Part 2: *managing time and place*, the best time for these tasks is when the brain is fresh and undistracted.

manageable chunks of up to 10 items!

This is similar to the paraphrasing strategy

Look & Say	→	Cover	→	Write	→	Check
look at the word and hear it by saying it aloud; perhaps stress the syllables so that you identify them		cover the word		write it from memory (visualise it and hear it)		check to see if you spelled it correctly. If not, repeat several times.

Useful grammar resources

Ascher, A 1993, *Think about editing: a grammar editing guide for ESL writers*, Heinle & Heinle, Boston.

Barry, AK 2002, *English grammar: language as human behaviour*, 2nd edn, Prentice Hall, Upper Saddle River, NJ.

Collerson, J 1994, *English grammar: a functional approach*, PETA, Newtown, NSW.

Collins COBUILD English grammar 2005, 2nd edn, HarperCollins, Glasgow. (advanced level)

Collins COBUILD student's dictionary plus grammar 2005, 3rd edn, HarperCollins, Glasgow. (intermediate level). See also CDROMs in this series.

Fowler, HR & Aaron, JE 2007, *The little, brown handbook*, 10th edn, Pearson Longman, New York. See also *http://www.pearsonhighered.com/littlebrown/*

academic writing is . . .
different things to different people:
a final word

Academic writing has different meanings for different people – students, their teachers and academic researchers and theorists – so that giving advice to students beginning as writers in the academy is problematic at this time. The practices of academic writing are being increasingly theorised, with debates and tensions as meanings are contested, and as 'taken-for-granted' assumptions about what counts as 'good' academic writing are scrutinised.[1] These debates are taking place in the rapidly changing 21st century, with the increasingly familiar description of challenges posed by globalisation and changes to work, the means of communication and so-called knowledge explosion of vast but often undifferentiated information on the Internet. Such changes have been described as 'the new orders' (Street 2004, p.10 -13) creating 'new kinds of people' (Gee 2008, p. 23). As van Leeuwen (2009b, p. 36) argues, such changes can also produce 'new writing'. In this context, for an educated person academic language is 'now at best a necessary, but not a sufficient condition for success in society' (Gee 2004, p.94) – being adaptive and open to new knowledge and new means of communication is also increasingly essential. These considerations have to be part of defining just what academic writing is.

To beginning students in this challenging context, however, academic writing primarily means assessment tasks, on which will depend marks, grades, maybe pass or failure in a subject, a course or progression to a higher degree. As student populations become increasingly diverse, it may also mean unlearning writing practices that were appropriate in a previous situation, such as school, work or another linguistic culture.[2] It is not surprising then that many students define academic writing in terms of uncertainty and frustration as they navigate between subjects, courses and disciplines and discover contrasting expectations in a university that is more a collection of diverse cultures than a single entity. It is therefore 'necessary', using Gee's term, for students first to learn how to write to meet the expectations of their discipline. From that point it is essential to develop a repertoire of writing skills to meet current challenges, both within and beyond the university. This requires practising critical analysis and reflection, to come to understand themselves as writers in changing contexts, knowing when and how to switch styles and genres (and within genres), according to specific purposes and audiences, and recognising the implications of doing so. It may also lead to taking a position among alternatives (Lea & Street 1998; Ivanic 2004). For 'success in society' (Gee 2004, p. 94) then, academic writing includes being adaptive and flexible in this way.

Among teachers in the university, both in discipline-specific and language-specific fields, there is probably consensus that in whatever form, academic writing should have clarity of language, predictability of structure, and honesty in substantiating any claims. Among those academics who assess students' writing and those who teach about it, however, there are considerably diverse definitions of what academic writing is and what it does, or should do, depending on conventions and traditions, discipline-specific genres and styles (Candlin & Plum 1998; Clerehan, Moore & Vance 2001; Fairclough 2009; Hyland 2002; Lea & Street 2006). To overcome the difficulties this may create for students, there is increasing collaboration between specialists to integrate academic writing teaching into the context of the discipline. Academics' expectations of students' writing are made more transparent by providing opportunities for discussion, demonstrations and models of what is valued in that discipline.[3] Students cannot expect this learning to be static, however. Increasingly, hybrid texts emerge in response to changing circumstances. The vocationally-driven demands of the modern university and rapid technological advances which add images, sound and interactivity to the written word may contest traditional forms of academic writing (Gee 2009; Henderson & Hirst 2007; Kress & van Leeuwen 2001; Street 2004; van Leeuwen 2009b). Being critically aware, in a positive sense, of past traditions and current challenges enables students to develop flexibility as well as essential professional writing competence.

Deciding the approach to take in this book meant listening to my own advice about being clear on purpose and audience, that is, to answer the questions that beginning writers ask. Therefore the first consideration for beginning writers in the university is to learn what is 'necessary'. Hence the choice of the practical 'how to' genre,[4] with the proviso of always checking specific requirements and asking questions. However, as has been demonstrated, there are 'no singular, unified practices that count always and only as academic literacy' (Henderson & Hirst 2007, p.26), so advice should not stop there (MacKay 2004; van Leeuwen 2009a). Instead, a multilayered approach has been attempted (Ivanic 2004), borrowing Lea and Street's definitions of approaches to academic writing (1998, 2006). This book thus contains a touch of the 'study skills approach', explaining expectations of a surface variety, and a liberal serving of the 'academic socialisation approach' to make cultural 'rules' and conventions more transparent, mixed with a generous amount of the text-based approach in examining particular academic genres. This is not to suggest that students' academic writing is a set of problems to be solved, or a way to apprentice them unquestioningly into their field armed with some fixed formulae of writing specifications. After all, to write like a historian or like an engineer oversimplifies the diversity of historians and engineers and the sorts of writing that they do (Baynham 2002). In contrast, the 'academic literacies approach' alerts students to the differences of multiple academic writing practices. By explaining and demonstrating the 'what' and 'how' of academic writing in terms of asking 'why' (and 'so what'), it is hoped that students become more critical, flexible and adaptive, recognising when and how to switch their writing according to audiences and purposes, understanding and questioning the 'who' of the writing. This includes reflecting on themselves as writers and participants in their field (Ivanic 1998).

Doubtless academic writing will always mean different things to different people as definitions and expectations of what makes 'good' academic writing continue to be debated and contested across a range of disciplines to reinforce, modify or change practices and beliefs. Such debates can be expected to proliferate as the rate of change and 'newness' accelerates. For students this requires understanding and utilising current accepted practices, a critical awareness of new realities and becoming adept at writing in a widening variety of ways for different purposes and audiences. This may be what academic writing is.

for further reading:

1. For examples of these debates, see Allwright, Clark & Marshall-Lee 1996; Baynham 2002; Candlin & Plum 1998; Fairclough 2009; Hyland 2002; Lea & Street 1998, 2006; Lee 1997; McLoughlin 1995; Pennycook 1997; Street 2004; van Leeuwen 2009b; Ivanic 1998, 2004.

2. For a range of examples of specific student situations see:
   » Indigenous students: McIntyre et al. 1996
   » Students from school: Clerehan, Moore & Vance 2001
   » Students with English as a second language: Hyland 2002; MacKay 2003; Power, Carmichael & Goldsmith 2007; Zamel & Spack 1998
   » Mature age students: Henderson, Noble & De George-Walker 2009; Lea 1993
   » Non-traditional students: Henderson & Hirst 2007; Street 2004.

3. For an example, see *Undergraduate study manual* 2008, Faculty of Nursing, Midwifery & Health, UTS; see also Lea & Street 2006. For reports of collaboration see Gordon, Baynham, Lee & San Miguel 1996, Lee 1997 and Trigwell & Yasukawa 1999. For another approach, see Henderson, Noble & De George-Walker 2009.

4. Among many popular examples, see Brown & Hood 1989; Clanchy & Ballard 1981; Davis & McKay 1996; Oshima & Hogue 1991; Peters 1985; Swales & Feak 1994.

reference list

Allwright, J, Clark, C & Marshall-Lee, A 1996, 'Developing a critical approach to study', *Review of ELT*, vol. 6, no. 1, pp. 71-81.

Baynham, M 2002, 'Academic writing in new and emergent discipline areas', in R Harrison, F Reeve, A Hanson & J Clarke (eds), *Supporting lifelong learning: vol. 1 perspectives on learning*, Routledge, London, pp. 188-202.

Brown, K & Hood, S 1989, *Writing matters: writing skills and strategies for students of English*, Cambridge University Press, Cambridge.

Candlin, CN & Plum, GA (eds) 1998, *Researching academic literacies*, Macquarie University, Sydney.

Clanchy, J & Ballard, C 1981, *Essay writing for students*, Longman Cheshire, Melbourne.

Clerehan, R, Moore, T & Vance, S 2001, 'Collaborating in the transition to tertiary writing', paper presented to *Meeting at the Crossroads, 18th Annual Conference of the Australasian Society for Computers in Learning in Tertiary Education*, Melbourne, 9-12 December, viewed 25 July 2009 <http://www.ascilite.org.au/conferences/melbourne01/pdf/papers/clerehanr.pdf>.

Davis, L & McKay, S 1996, *Structures and strategies: an introduction to academic writing*, Macmillan Education Australia, South Melbourne.

Fairclough, N 2009, 'A dialectical-relational approach to critical discourse analysis in social research', in R Wodak & M Meyer (eds), *Methods of critical discourse*, Sage Publications, London, pp. 162-186.

Gee, JP 2004, *Situated language and learning: a critique of traditional schooling*, Routledge, New York.

Gee, JP 2008, 'Literacies, schools, and kinds of people in the new capitalism', in TL McCarty (ed.), *Language, literacy and power in schooling*, Lawrence Erlbaum Associates, Mahwah, NJ, pp. 223-240.

Gee, JP 2009, 'Digital media and learning as an emerging field, part 1: how we got here', *International Journal of Learning and Media*, vol. 1, no. 2, pp.13-23, viewed 21 July 2009, <http://www.mitpressjournals.org/doi/full/10.1162/ijlm.2009.0011#h2>.

Gordon, K, Baynham, M, Lee, A & San Miguel, C 1996, 'Academic writing and disciplinary politics: what every student needs to know', paper presented to *Knowledge and Discourse Conference*, University of Hong Kong, 18-21 June.

Henderson, R & Hirst, E 2007, 'Reframing academic literacy: re-examining a short-course for "disadvantaged" tertiary students', *English Teaching: Practice and Critique*, vol. 6, no. 2, pp. 25-38, viewed 20 July 2009, <http://education.waikato.ac.nz/research/files/etpc/2007v6n2art2.pdf>.

Henderson, R, Noble, K & DeGeorge-Walker, L 2009, 'Transitioning into university: "interrupted" first year students problem solving their way into study', *Studies in Learning, Evaluation, Innovation and Development*, vol. 6, no. 1, pp. 51-64, viewed 20 July 2009, <http://sleid.cqu.edu.au/viewissue.php?id=19#Refereed_Articles>.

Hyland, K 2002, 'Specificity revisited: how far should we go?' *English for Specific Purposes*, vol. 21, issue 4, pp. 385-395.

Ivanic, R 1998, *Writing and identity: the discoursal construction of identity in academic writing*, John Benjamins, Amsterdam.

Ivanic, R 2004, 'Discourses of writing and learning to write', *Language and Education*, vol. 18, no. 3, pp. 220-245.

Kress, G and van Leeuwen, T 2001, *Multimodal discourse: the modes and media of contemporary communication*, Arnold, London.

Lea, M 1993, '"I thought I could write until I came here": student writing in higher education', in D Graddol & S Thomas (eds), *Language in a Changing Europe*, British Association for Applied Linguistics, Sept, pp. 64-72.

Lea, M & Street, B 1998, 'Student writing in higher education: an academic literacies approach', *Studies in Higher Education*, vol. 23, no. 2, pp. 157-172.

Lea, M & Street, B 2006, 'The "academic literacies" model: theory and application', *Theory Into Practice*, vol. 45, no. 4, viewed 21 July 2009, <http://www3.unisul.br/paginas/ensino/pos/linguagem/cd/English/22i.pdf>.

Lee, A 1997, 'Working together? Academic literacies, co-production and professional partnerships', *Literacy and Numeracy Studies*, vol. 7, no. 2, pp. 65-82.

MacKay, T 2003, 'Gee's theory of D/discourse and research in teaching English as a second language: implications for the mainstream', paper presented to *Theory, Culture and Discourse in Education: Education Graduate Student Symposium*, University of Manitoba, 14-15 March, viewed 25 July 2009, http://www.umanitoba.ca/educ/symposium03/documents/MacKay03.pdf.

McIntyre, J, Ardler, W, Morley-Warner, T, Solomon, N & Spindler, L 1996, *Culture matters: factors affecting the outcomes of participation in vocational education and training by Australian Indigenous peoples*, Research Centre for Vocational Education and Training, University of Technology, Sydney.

McLoughlin, C 1995, 'Tertiary literacy: a constructivist perspective', *Open Letter*, vol. 5, no. 2, pp. 27-42.

Oshima, A & Hogue, A 1991, *Writing academic English*, 2nd edn, Addison-Wesley, New York.

Pennycook, A 1997, 'Vulgar pragmatism, critical pragmatism and EAP', *English for Specific Purposes*, vol. 16, no. 4, pp. 253-270.

Peters, P 1985, *Strategies for student writers: a guide to writing essays, tutorial papers, exam papers and reports*, John Wiley & Sons, Brisbane.

Power, C, Carmichael, E & Goldsmith R 2007, 'Parrot poo on the windscreen: metaphor in academic skills learning', *Journal of Academic Language and Learning*, vol. 1, no. 1, pp. A.18-A.32, viewed 21 July 2009, <http://journal.aall.org.au/index.php/jall/article/view/31/44>.

Street, B 2004, 'Academic literacies and the "new orders": implications for research and practice in student writing in higher education', *Learning and Teaching in the Social Sciences*, vol. 1, issue 1, pp. 9-20, viewed 25 July 2009, <http://www.ucl.ac.uk/cishe/downloads/BrianStreet/BrianStreet%20Debates%20in%20HE%20UCL%2007.pdf>.

Swales, J M & Feak, C B 1994, *Academic writing for graduate students: a course for non-native speakers of English*, University of Michigan Press, Ann Arbor.

Trigwell, K & Yasukawa, K 1999, 'Learning in a graduate attributes-based engineering course', paper presented to *HERDSA Annual International Conference*, Melbourne, 12-15 July, viewed 26 July 2009, <http://www.herdsa.org.au/wp-content/uploads/conference/1999/pdf/Trigwell.PDF>.

Undergraduate study manual 2008, Version 1.3, Faculty of Nursing, Midwifery and Health, University of Technology, Sydney, viewed 13 August 2009, <http://www.nmh.uts.edu.au/students/current/documents-policies/ug-study-manual-may08.pdf>.

van Leeuwen, T 2009a, 'Discourse as the recontextualisation of social practice: a guide', in R Wodak & M Meyer (eds), *Methods of critical discourse analysis*, Sage Publications, London, pp. 144-161.

van Leeuwen, T 2009b, 'The new writing', *Tower. UTS: Alumni*, Issue 1, Winter, p.36.

Zamel V & Spack R (eds) 1998, *Negotiating academic literacies: teaching and learning across cultures*, Lawrence Erlbaum Associates, Mahwah, NJ.

bibliography

Allwright, J, Clark, C & Marshall-Lee, A 1996, 'Developing a critical approach to study', *Review of ELT*, vol. 6, no. 1, pp. 71-81.

American Psychological Association, 2001, *Publication manual of the American Psychological Association*, 5th edn, Washington DC.

Ascher, A 1993, *Think about editing: a grammar editing guide for ESL writers*, Heinle & Heinle, Boston, MA.

Australian Government Publishing Service 1997, *Stylewise*, vol. 2, no. 3.

Australian Government Publishing Service 1997, *Stylewise*, vol. 3, no. 3.

Ball, CC, Dice, L & Bartholomae, D 1990, 'Telling secrets: students, readers and disciplinary authorities', in R Beach & S Hynds (eds), *Developing discourse practices in adolescence and adulthood*, Ablex Publishing, Norwood, NJ, pp. 337-358.

Barry, AK 2002, *English grammar: language as human behaviour*, 2nd edn, Prentice Hall, Upper Saddle River, NJ.

Barton, D 1992, 'The social nature of writing', in D Barton & S Padmore (eds), *Writing in the community*, Sage Publications, London, pp. 1-13.

Baylis, P & Knapp, P 1990, *Report writing in the professional workplace*, Institute of Languages, UNSW, Sydney.

Baynham, M 1995, *Literacy practices: investigating literacy in social contexts*, Longman, London.

Baynham, M 2000, 'Academic writing in new and emergent discipline areas', in M Lea & B Stierer (eds), *Student writing in higher education: new contexts*, The Society for Research into Higher Education and Open University Press, Buckingham, pp. 17-31.

Baynham, M 2002, 'Academic writing in new and emergent discipline areas', in R Harrison, F Reeve, A Hanson & J Clarke (eds), *Supporting lifelong learning: vol. 1 perspectives on learning*, Routledge, London, pp. 188-202.

Baynham, M, Beck, D, Gordon, K, Lee, A & San Miguel, C 1995, 'Constructing a discourse position: quoting, referring and attribution in academic writing', in K Chanock (ed.), *Integrating the teaching of academic discourse into courses in the disciplines: proceedings of the 1994 Language and Academic Skills Conference*, La Trobe University, Melbourne, pp. 8-18.

Bennett, TJ (ed.) 2009, *Referencing guide*, 11th edn, Edith Cowan University, Mt Lawley, viewed 6 March 2009, <http://www.ecu.edu.au/CLT/pdf/refguide.pdf>.

Blanton, L 1987, 'Reshaping ESL students' perceptions of writing', *ELT Journal*, no. 41, pp. 112-118.

Brennan, MJ 1995, 'Essay writing in nursing: alerting students and teachers to the educational benefits', *Nurse Education Today*, 1, Pearson Professional, vol. 1, pp. 351-356.

Brown, A 1999, 'The case for generic skills tuition', *HERDSA News*, March, pp. 21-23.

Brown, K & Hood, S 1989, *Writing matters: writing skills and strategies for students of English*, Cambridge University Press.

Brown, R 1997, 'How did we get a literacy problem in research articles?' in Z Golebiowski (ed.), *Policy and practice of tertiary literacy: selected proceedings of the First National Conference on Tertiary Literacy: Research and Practice*, vol. 1, Victoria University of Technology, Melbourne, pp. 82-95.

Candlin, CN 1998, 'Researching writing in the academy: participants, texts, processes and practices', in CN Candlin & GA Plum (eds), *Researching academic literacies*, Macquarie University, Sydney.

Candlin, CN & Plum, GA (eds) 1998, *Researching academic literacies*, Macquarie University, Sydney.

Chanock, K (ed.) 1995, *Integrating the teaching of academic discourse into courses in the disciplines: proceedings of the 1994 Language and Academic Skills Conference*, La Trobe University, Melbourne.

Chapman, J 1983, *Reading development and cohesion*, Heinemann Educational, London.

Chicago manual of style: for authors, editors and copywriters, 1993, 14th edn, University of Chicago Press, Chicago.

Clanchy, J & Ballard, C 1981, *Essay writing for students*, Longman Cheshire, Melbourne.

Clark, R 1995, 'Developing critical reading practices', *Prospect, a Journal of Australian TESOL*, vol. 10, no. 2, July, pp. 65-80.

Clark, R & Ivanic, R 1997, *The politics of writing*, Routledge, London.

Clerehan, R, Moore, T & Vance, S 2001, 'Collaborating in the transition to tertiary writing', paper presented to *Meeting at the Crossroads, 18th Annual Conference of the Australasian Society for Computers in Learning in Tertiary Education*, Melbourne, 9-12 December, viewed 25 July 2009 <http://www.ascilite.org.au/conferences/melbourne01/pdf/papers/clerehanr.pdf>.

Collerson, J 1994, *English grammar: a functional approach*, PETA, Newtown, NSW.

Collins COBUILD English grammar 2005, 2nd edn, Harper Collins, Glasgow.

Collins COBUILD student's dictionary plus grammar 2005, 3rd edn, Harper Collins, Glasgow.

Davis, L & McKay, S 1996, *Structures and strategies: an introduction to academic writing*, Macmillan Education Australia, South Melbourne.

Derewianka, B 1990, *Exploring how texts work*, PETA, Rozelle, NSW.

Drury, H & Webb, C 1991, 'Teaching academic writing at the tertiary level', *Prospect, a Journal of Australian TESOL*, vol. 7, pp. 7-27.

Eagleson, RD 1991, *Writing in Plain English*, AGPS, Canberra.

Fairclough, NL 1989, *Language and power*, Longman, London.

Fairclough, NL 1992, *Discourse and social change*, Polity Press, Cambridge.

Fairclough, NL (ed.) 1992, *Critical language awareness*, Longman, London.

Fairclough, NL 1995, *Critical discourse analysis: the critical study of language*, Longman, London.

Fairclough, N 2009, 'A dialectical-relational approach to critical discourse analysis in social research', in R Wodak & M Meyer (eds), *Methods of critical discourse*, Sage Publications, London, pp. 162-186.

Faigley, L 1992, *Fragments of rationality: postmodernity and the subject of composition*, University of Pittsburgh Press.

Fathman, AK. & Whalley, E 1990, 'Teacher response to student writing: focus on form versus content', in B Kroll (ed.), *Second language writing: research insights for the classroom*, Cambridge University Press.

Fowler, HR & Aaron, JE 2007, *The little, brown handbook*, 10th edn, Pearson Longman, New York.

Gee, JP 2004, *Situated language and learning: a critique of traditional schooling*, Routledge, New York.

Gee, JP 2008, 'Literacies, schools, and kinds of people in the new capitalism', in TL McCarty (ed.), *Language, literacy and power in schooling*, Lawrence Erlbaum Associates, Mahwah, NJ, pp. 223-240.

Gee, JP 2008, *Social linguistics and literacies: ideology in discourses*, 3rd edn, Taylor & Francis, London.

Gee, JP 2009, 'Digital media and learning as an emerging field, part 1: how we got here', *International Journal of Learning and Media*, vol. 1, no. 2, pp.13-23, viewed 21 July 2009, <http://www.mitpressjournals.org/doi/full/10.1162/ijlm.2009.0011#h2>.

Golebiowski, Z & Borland, H (eds) 1997, *Academic communication across disciplines and cultures. Selected proceedings of the first national conference on tertiary literacy: research and practice*, vol. 2, Victoria University of Technology, Melbourne, pp. 294-293.

Gordon, K, Baynham, M, Lee, A & San Miguel, C 1996, 'Academic writing and disciplinary politics: what every student needs to know', paper presented to *Knowledge and Discourse Conference*, University of Hong Kong, 18-21 June.

Grabe, W & Kaplan, RB 1996, *Theory and practice of writing*, Longman, New York.

Guide to writing assignments. UTS: Business 2006, Faculty of Business, University of Technology, Sydney.

Guide to writing assignments. UTS: Business 2006, Faculty of Business, University of Technology, Sydney, viewed 6 March 2009, <http://www.business.uts.edu.au/teaching/guide/guide.pdf>.

Halliday, MAK & Hasan, R 1976, *Cohesion in English*, Longman, London.

Halliday, MAK & Hasan, R 1985, *Language, context and text: aspects of language in a social semiotic perspective*, Deakin University Press, Melbourne.

Hammond, J, Burns, A, Joyce, H, Brosnan, D & Gerot, L 1992, *English for social purposes*, NCELTR, Sydney.

Harvard Referencing. The 'in-text' system n.d., Learning Centre, University of NSW, viewed 6 March 2009, <http://www.lc.unsw.edu.au/onlib/ref.html>.

Heimlich, JE & Pittelman, SD 1986, *Semantic mapping: classroom applications*, International Reading Association, Newark, DE.

Henderson, R & Hirst, E 2007, 'Reframing academic literacy: re-examining a short-course for "disadvantaged" tertiary students', *English Teaching: Practice and Critique*, vol. 6, no. 2, pp. 25-38, viewed 20 July 2009, <http://education.waikato.ac.nz/research/files/etpc/2007v6n2art2.pdf>.

Henderson, R, Noble, K & DeGeorge-Walker, L 2009, 'Transitioning into university: "interrupted" first year students problem solving their way into study', *Studies in Learning, Evaluation, Innovation and Development*, vol. 6, no. 1, pp. 51-64, viewed 20 July 2009, <http://sleid.cqu.edu.au/viewissue.php?id=19#Refereed_Articles>.

Hodge, R & Kress, G 1993, *Language as ideology*, 2nd edn, Routledge, London.

Hyland, K 2002, 'Specificity revisited: how far should we go?' *English for Specific Purposes*, vol. 21, issue 4, pp. 385-395.

Ivanic, R 1998, *Writing and identity: the discoursal construction of identity in academic writing*, John Benjamins, Amsterdam.

Ivanic, R 2004, 'Discourses of writing and learning to write', *Language and Education*, vol. 18, no. 3, pp. 220-245.

Ivanic, R & Simpson, J 1992, 'Who's who in academic writing?' in NL Fairclough (ed.), *Critical language awareness*, Longman, London.

Joyce, H 1992, *Workplace texts in the language classroom*, NSW AMES, Sydney.

Kress, G 1985, *Linguistic processes in sociocultural practice*, Deakin University Press, Melbourne.

Kress, G & Hodge, R 1979, *Language as ideology*, Routledge, London.

Kress, G and van Leeuwen, T 2001, *Multimodal discourse: the modes and media of contemporary communication*, Arnold, London.

Lankshear, C 1994, *Critical literacy: occasional paper 3*, Australian Curriculum Studies Association, Belconnen, ACT.

Lea, M 1993, '"I thought I could write until I came here": student writing in higher education', in D Graddol & S Thomas (eds), *Language in a Changing Europe*, British Association for Applied Linguistics, Sept., pp. 64-72.

Lea M & Stierer B (eds) 2000, *Student writing in higher education: new contexts*, The Society for Research into Higher Education and Open University Press, Buckingham.

Lea, M & Street, B 1998, 'Student writing in higher education: an academic literacies approach', *Studies in Higher Education*, vol. 23, no. 2, pp. 157-172.

Lea, M & Street, B 2006, 'The "academic literacies" model: theory and application', *Theory Into Practice*, vol. 45, no. 4, viewed 21 July 2009, <http://www3.unisul.br/paginas/ensino/pos/linguagem/cd/English/22i.pdf>.

Lee, A 1997, 'Working together? Academic literacies, co-production and professional partnerships', *Literacy and Numeracy Studies*, vol. 7, no. 2, pp. 65-82.

Lee, A, Baynham, M, Beck, D, Gordon, K & San Miguel, C 1995, 'Researching discipline specific academic literacy practices: some methodological issues', *Research and Development in Higher Education*, no. 18, pp. 464-482.

MacKay, T 2003, 'Gee's theory of D/discourse and research in teaching English as a second language: implications for the mainstream', paper presented to *Theory, Culture and Discourse in Education: Education Graduate Student Symposium*, University of Manitoba, 14-15 March, viewed 25 July 2009, http://www.umanitoba.ca/educ/symposium03/documents/MacKay03.pdf.

Mahony, D 1997, *The student guide for writing and studying effectively at university: the world of ideas and the world of text*, Queensland University of Technology, Brisbane.

McIntyre, J, Ardler, W, Morley-Warner, T, Solomon, N & Spindler, L 1996, *Culture matters: factors affecting the outcomes of participation in vocational education and training by Australian Indigenous peoples*, Research Centre for Vocational Education and Training, University of Technology, Sydney.

McLoughlin, C 1995, 'Tertiary literacy: a constructivist perspective', *Open Letter*, vol. 5, no. 2, pp. 27-42.

Miller, BK 1994, 'The literature review', in G LoBiondo-Wood & J Haber (eds), *Nursing research: methods, critical appraisal, and utilization*, 3rd edn, Mosby, St Louis, MO.

Modern Language Association of America, *MLA handbook for writers of research papers 2009*, 7th edn, New York.

Morris, A 1987, 'Effective reading in content areas', *Reading around series*, no. 2, Australian Reading Association, Carlton South.

Muspratt, S, Luke, A & Freebody, P (eds) 1997, *Constructing critical literacies: teaching and learning textual practice*, Allen and Unwin, St Leonards, NSW.

Oshima, A & Hogue, A 1991, *Writing academic English*, 2nd edn, Addison-Wesley, New York.

Pennycook, A 1994, 'Beyond (F)utilitarianism: English as academic purpose', *Hong Kong Papers in Linguistics and Language Teaching*, vol. 17, pp. 11-21.

Pennycook, A 1997, 'Vulgar pragmatism, critical pragmatism and EAP', *English for Specific Purposes*, vol. 16, no. 4, pp. 253-270.

Percy, D 1989, *Adult study tactics; a springboard to learning*, Macmillan, Melbourne.

Peters, P (ed.) 1999, *Australian style, a national bulletin*, vol. 7, no. 2.

Peters, P 1985, *Strategies for student writers: a guide to writing essays, tutorial papers, exam papers and reports*, John Wiley & Sons, Brisbane.

Piaget, J 1926, *The language and thought of the child*, Routledge & Keegan Paul, London.

Power, C, Carmichael, E & Goldsmith R 2007, 'Parrot poo on the windscreen: metaphor in academic skills learning', *Journal of Academic Language and Learning*, vol. 1, no. 1, pp. A.18-A.32, viewed 21 July 2009, <http://journal.aall.org.au/index.php/jall/article/view/31/44>.

Rolfe, G 1997, 'Writing ourselves: creating knowledge in a postmodern world', *Nurse Education Today*, 17, Harcourt Brace, pp. 442-448.

Street, B 1999, 'Position paper: new directions in literacy research', paper presented to *Academic Literacies, International Association of Applied Linguistics Symposium*, viewed 10 November 1999, <http://www.education.uts.edu.au/AILA>.

Street, B 2004, 'Academic literacies and the "new orders": implications for research and practice in student writing in higher education', *Learning and Teaching in the Social Sciences*, vol. 1, issue 1, pp. 9-20, viewed 25 July 2009, <http://www.ucl.ac.uk/cishe/downloads/BrianStreet/BrianStreet%20Debates%20in%20HE%20UCL%2007.pdf>.

Style manual for authors, editors and printers 2002, 6th edn, John Wiley and Sons Australia, Milton, Queensland.

Swales JM & Feak, CB 1994, *Academic writing for graduate students: a course for non-native speakers of English*, University of Michigan Press.

The Australian concise Oxford dictionary 2004, 4th edn, Oxford University Press, South Melbourne.

The Macquarie dictionary 2009, 4th edn, Macquarie Dictionary, Sydney.

Trigwell, K & Yasukawa, K 1999, 'Learning in a graduate attributes-based engineering course', paper presented to *HERDSA Annual International Conference*, Melbourne, 12-15 July, viewed 26 July 2009, <http://www.herdsa.org.au/wp-content/uploads/conference/1999/pdf/Trigwell.PDF>.

Undergraduate study manual 2008, Version 1.3, Faculty of Nursing, Midwifery and Health, University of Technology, Sydney, viewed 13 August 2009, <http://www.nmh.uts.edu.au/students/current/documents-policies/ug-study-manual-may08.pdf>.

van Leeuwen, T 2009a, 'Discourse as the recontextualisation of social practice: a guide', in R Wodak & M Meyer (eds), *Methods of critical discourse analysis*, Sage Publications, London, pp. 144-161.

van Leeuwen, T 2009b, 'The new writing', *Tower. UTS: Alumni*, Issue 1, Winter, p.36.

Wallace, C 1992, 'Critical literacy awareness in the EFL classroom', in NL Fairclough (ed.), *Critical language awareness*, Longman, London.

Webb, C (ed.) 1991, *Writing an essay in the humanities and social sciences*, Learning Assistance Centre, University of Sydney.

Webb, C & Drury, H 1991, The literacy needs of students in higher education, position paper in F Christie (ed.), *Teaching English literacy: a project of national significance on the pre-service preparation of teachers for teaching English literacy*, DEET, Canberra.

Wells, G 1991, 'Apprenticeship in literacy', in C Walsh (ed.), *Literacy as praxis: culture, language and pedagogy*, Ablex Publishing, Norwood, NJ.

Weissberg, R & Buker, S 1990, *Writing up research*, Prentice-Hall Regents, Englewood Cliffs, NJ.

Zamel, V 1982, 'Writing: the process of discovering meaning', *TESOL Quarterly*, vol. 6, no. 2, pp. 195-208.

Zamel V & Spack R (eds) 1998, *Negotiating academic literacies: teaching and learning across cultures*, Lawrence Erlbaum Associates, Mahwah, NJ.

appendix

key words in interpreting a task

account for	give reasons for, explain
analyse	examine each part of an issue or argument
argue	propose and support a point of view, or weigh up and compare several views on an issue, develop a thesis
assess	make a judgment weighing up positive and negative features
compare	show the similarities and differences
contrast	emphasise the differences between
critically analyse	examine the parts (as above), weighing up positive and negative features
critically evaluate	make a judgment weighing up positive and negative features
criticise	analyse and make a judgment weighing up positive and negative features
critique	as above
describe	tell about features, factors, qualities, aspects
define	set out the meaning (of a term, word); describe (sometimes explain)
discuss	in the sense of account for; also to weigh up and compare several views on an issue, develop a thesis
enumerate	specify and list the main features, one by one
evaluate	make a judgement on the worth, truth or usefulness etc. weighing up positive and negative features
explain	give reasons for, clarify cause and effect, reason and result
indicate	point out and list the main features, factors
identify	select and list the main features, factors
illustrate	make clear, give examples
interpret	explain what is meant and relate to the topic
justify	give reasons
outline	list the main or general points
	(give a) rationale for
	give reasons, explain why
review	in the sense of giving a list, an overview; also to make a critical analysis
summarise	give a succinct description
synthesise	bring parts of an analysis together in a new perspective

index

abstract (report) 11, 50–55, 74–75
abstract noun 63, 65, 68, 69
acronyms 50, 59, 68
active construction 60–61, 63, 67
AGPS style 84, 87, 94, 95, 100
agreement, subject and verb 46, 70, 99–100
aim (report) 55, 57, 74
analysis 11, 21, 37–45, 50–57, 66, 68, 74, 77–80, 90, 106, *app*
annotated bibliography 75–76, 82
apostrophe 101–103
appendix, appendices 54, 57–60
argument 10–11, 15, 25–30, 36, 42–48, 57, 68, 70, 79, 85, 91, *app*
assessment criteria 21
balance 15, 21, 29, 42, 70–71, 78
bias 71, 76
bibliography 48, 51, 54, 59–60, 84, 87–88, 93–94
body 11, 34–37, 41, 46, 56–60, 80
brainstorm 22–23, 30, 38, 41, 53
case study 14, 68, 70, 76–78,
cause and effect 38–39, 116
checklist: essay 48
checklist: last draft 32
checklist: report 60
citation 26, 78, 84–93
cohesion 24, 28–29, 36–37, 50
comparison-contrast 21, 37, 40–42
comparison table/grid 41, 44, 46, 77, 79, 80
comparison 52, 57, 82

conclusion 25, 28, 31, 34–36, 41, 44, 47–48, 74–78, 81
conclusion (report) 50–54, 58, 60
connections 28–31, 50, 64, 99
constructing a report 53–60
constructing an essay 34–48
critical analysis 11, 37, 42–45, 78–79, 106, *app*
critical evaluation 43, 78–79, *app*
critical review 79
critique 15, 43, 56, 76, 78, *app*
debate *see argument*
define, definition 13–14, 29–32, 37, 45, 52, 55, 59, 68, *app*
demons 103
describe, description 21, 37–43, 56–57, 70, 78–79, *app*
direct quote/citation 86, 91–92
discourse 50, 52, 72
discussion 13, 21, 35–48, 50, 53, 56–58, 69, 74, 77, 79, 82, *app*
discussion (report) 53–60
distance 44, 65–71
draft: final 24–25, 63, 65, 70
draft: first 24–25, 27, 30, 35, 63
drafting process 15, 18, 24, 44
e-communication 12, 88
editing process 12, 14, 18, 20, 24–25, 30
emotive language 64, 71
EndNote 22, 86, 93
endnote, endnotes 86–87, 93
essay structure 34–44
essay types 37–44
essay writing process 17–32, 34,
evaluation *see critical evaluation*
evaluative terms 21, 29
exam essay 29
executive summary 11, 50, 52, 58, 60, 74–75

experiential report   51
explanation   21, 37–43, 53, 71, 77, 90–91, 101
expository text   11, 37
feedback   14–15, 26
findings (report)   50–60, 74–75, 82, 101
final draft   *see draft: final*
first draft   *see draft: first*
flow   11, 23, 27, 31, 59, 91–92
flow chart   23, 53
focus   32, 35, 39, 52, 63–71, 80, 91
footnote, footnotes   86–87, 93
formal writing,   *see impersonal tone/writing*
free write   25, 35, 42, 44, 63
glossary   50, 54, 59, 68
grammar   24, 26, 30, 97–104
graphics (report)   56, 59
headings & subheadings   28–29, 31, 50–56, 75, 77, 82
illustrate   37, 50, *app*
impersonal tone/writing   14, 30, 38, 42, 52, 56–57, 63–70, 74, 100
incomplete sentences   98
indirect quotes/referencing   87
informal writing   *see personal writing*
information report   30, 51
initialisms   50, 68
integrating evidence   91
intelligent stranger   13–14, 25, 65
Internet   12, 75, 88, 92, 94–95
interpreting the task   20, 29
in-text citation   26, 78, 86–87
introduction   11, 27, 34–36, 41, 45, 48
introduction (report)   51, 53, 55, 59–60, 74, 80
issues paper   *see discussion*
its/it's   101–103
jargon   68

journal:
  personal   63–65, 81–82
  professional and research   72, 74, 75, 79, 84–85, 89, 93–95
key terms/words   22–23, 27–29, 31, 90, *app*
language choices/features   38, 40, 42, 44, 51–52, 56–58
learning contract   30
levels of academic writing   62
literature review   74, 76, 79–82
literature review (report)   50, 53, 55
major study   30
margin notes   22–23, 82, 90
method, methodology (report)   53, 56–57, 74, 82
mindmap   23–24, 37–38, 48, 53
model discussion essay   45–48
narrative   39, 63, 77, 81
nominalisation   65, 69
notemaking   22, 27
objective of a task   10, 21
objectives (report)   55, 57, 60
objectivity   44, 71
online referencing   19, 22, 64, 74, 84, 86, 88–89, 93–95
opinion   41, 85, 88, 92
organising information   21, 28–29, 31, 37
paragraph   11–12, 24–31, 34–38, 41, 46, 48, 54–55, 74, 77–80, 86–89, 91, 94
paragraph test   27
paraphrasing   48, 78, 87–91, 104
passive construction   56–57, 60, 63, 65, 67, 70
patterns of organisation   21, 37
pen-in-hand   22, 25, 29, 90
personal writing   62, 64, 70, 77, 81
plagiarism   12, 23, 67, 84, 90, 92–93
Plain English   15, 71
polishing   20, 26, 30

planning   20, 22, 26, 37–38, 41, 44, 46, 53, 78, 93
preliminary parts (report)   53–54
preview   34–35, 41, 45, 80
primary source   65, 79, 86, 88–89
pronouns   38, 40, 56–57, 63–64, 66–67, 70, 100, 102
proofreading   20, 26, 30, 36, 84, 92, 95, 97–104
punctuation   97–104
quoting   *see referencing, citations*
rationale   38, 53, 55, *app*
recommendations (report)   50–54, 57–58, 60
reference list   26, 51, 54, 59–60, 82, 84–89, 93–95
referencing   11, 24, 46–48, 75, 86–87, 93–95
reflecting, reflective journal   63–64, 73, 81
RefWorks   22, 86, 93
report writing   28, 30–31
report writing: sections   53–57
report writing: types   51–52
research report   52
research review   82
researching   18, 20, 22, 29, 93
restatement   28
review   34, 36–37, 44, 55, 79–80, *app*
routine   19
scope   23, 34, 39, 45, 51, 53, 55, 60, 79
secondary sources   79, 86, 88
sequencing   31, 38, 53, 56
sexist language   100
signal words   11, 17, 24, 27–29, 31–32, 38, 40, 42, 44, 48, 50, 54, 56, 74, 78–80, 98
sorting into a plan   20, 23, 29–30
sounding academic   25, 62–72
sources   *see referencing*
spelling   103–104

stages of writing process   20–26
structure of text   *see patterns of organisation, constructing an essay/report*
study space   19
style   14–15, 62–72
style manuals   54, 58–59, 71, 84–95
summary   *see executive summary,* 76, 79
supplementary parts (report)   53–54, 59
synopsis   74
synthesis   42, 80, *app*
table of contents (report)   31, 51, 54, 57–58, 60
tables   56–60
task words   21, 29
technical terms   15, 50, 65, 68
tense, verbs   38, 40, 42, 44, 51–52, 56–58, 60, 67, 78, 98, 101
tentative tone   65, 69, 70, 85
text types   11, 14, 63, 74–82
theme   24–25
thesis   11, 25, 34–36, 42–45, 47–48, 79–81, 89, *app*
time management   18–19
timeless/universal present tense   40, 44, 67, 101
tone   see style
topic sentences   11, 27–32, 38–40, 42, 44, 48, 54, 56, 78, 80
verbs   40, 65, 67–70, 99, 101, 104
word count   14, 25, 69, 79, 91
writer's block   18
writing process   18–32, 35